The Banking Swindle

Money Creation and the State
by
Kerry Bolton

The Banking Swindle

Money Creation and the State

by

Kerry Bolton

ISBN-13: 978-1-910881-65-1

Black House Publishing Ltd
Kemp House
152 City Road
London
United Kingdom
EC1V 2NX
www.blackhousepublishing.com
Email: info@blackhousepublishing.com

The study of money, above all other fields in economics, is one in which complexity is used to disguise truth or to evade truth, not to reveal it. The process by which banks create money is so simple the mind is repelled. With something so important, a deeper mystery seems only decent.

- Dr John Kenneth Galbraith,
American Economist and Presidential Adviser.

Contents

Contents

The Banking Swindle

Money Creation and the State
by
Kerry Bolton

Introduction

In the midst of the global debt crisis, with riots, bombings, default, and failed policies proposed from all sides of politics, the world is floundering about with less understanding of the problems and possible solutions than our 'less educated' parents and grand parents during the Great Depression. The scribbling and chattering classes have hardly helped; indeed they have obfuscated the character of economics and finance, and one might be tempted to conclude that is the job of many of them.

Eighty to ninety years ago our parents and grandparents understood what was needed in regard to the problems that descended upon them from 'above'. As the iconic New Zealand Labour politician John A Lee remarked in his pamphlets of the time, the problems of banking and the need for reform were understood and debated throughout the population, in pubs, on buses, at work… The people did not need a tertiary education in economics to understand what was wrong. People such as Lee and the New Zealand businessman and magazine proprietor Henry Kelliher explained the situation in the simple terms that are more sufficient than the explanations provided today by economists, with jargon that means nothing in real terms. The nationalisation of the New Zealand Reserve Bank, and the necessity of issuing state credit was the main platform that brought the First New Zealand Labour Government to Office in 1935. The Government dealt with the Depression not by outmoded socialist theories from the 19th century, but by intervening in the key area of banking. The impetus for this had not come from Marxists, who opposed Lee's efforts, but from the burgeoning Social Credit movement that had emerged over the British Dominions. Banking reform had been promulgated successfully by two men of the 'Right', the above named Kelliher, and the then well known banking reformer A N Field, whose books, such as *The Truth About the Slump*, became best-sellers in 1930s New Zealand. The same year, (1935) Social Credit assumed Office in Alberta, Canada.

Throughout the Western world, in the aftermath of World War I, a decade prior to the Great Depression, there was widespread demand for banking reform. This demand was more likely to come from the Right than from the moribund Left, which could not think much beyond taxation and nationalisation (like the present 'Occupy Movement' in response to the current debt crisis). Indeed, in Germany, that nation's leading banking reformer, Gottfried Feder, attempted to interest the short-lived Soviet Republic in Bavaria in his plans for banking reform, only to be rebuffed, but finding a ready audience in the embryonic German Workers' Party, which fifteen years later partially implemented the Feder plan and set Germany on the course to recovery amidst world Depression.

Now the whole parasitic debt finance system totters and falls like a house of cards, as the greed of bad investments based on usury captures up with the money-lenders. In the USA, Ireland and Spain the crisis was precipitated by mortgage lending, which could not be sustained. The common folk in indebting themselves while not receiving sufficient income to keep up mortgage repayments and sundry other debts, went bust, which ran down through the entire financial system, causing state defaults in some instances, while other states sell their assets to pay off their debts. Hence, for example, Greece gave away her income from Airport fees and lotteries to Goldman Sachs in exchange for hiding Greek debt from European Union auditors. The international banks meanwhile are bailed out by Governments, which should instead be releasing the money directly to their people.

Jerome L Stein, Emeritus Professor Economics, Brown University, in referring to the origins of the Irish debt crisis, explained the situation, which also relates to the global debt crisis in general:

> The growing construction boom was financed by Irish banks which in turn were financed by external financial markets where inexpensive funds were available. In the last four years of the boom from 2003 onward banks competed aggressively in the mortgage markets with little regard for the creditworthiness of the mortgagors. At the end of 2003, net indebtedness of Irish banks to the world was over 10 percent of GDP. By 2008, borrowing mainly for property jumped to over 60 percent of GDP. Even before the failure of Lehman Brothers in September 2008, Irish residential properties had been falling for more than 18 months. At no point throughout the period—even as the crisis neared—did the Central Bank of Ireland, and the Financial Services Authority staff believe that any of the institutions were facing serious underlying difficulties, let alone insolvency problems? When the crisis occurred, the collapse of construction and the fall in property prices led to the insolvency of banks. Their net worth vanished. The state took large equity stakes in most banks and issued government guaranteed bonds. Although Ireland's public debt immediately prior to the crisis was low, the fiscal deficit and public sector borrowing surged. The primary reason for the surge in the deficit was the collapse of tax revenues in 2008–09 due to the collapse of the housing sector.[1]

In whatever state one looks, as this book shows, the destabilising factor ultimately rests with the parasitism of the private banking system based on DEBT.

This book is based on a series of articles written during 2010-2012 for sundry journals. The material has been heavily re-written, adapted, supplemented and reorganised. In the midst of

---

[1] '*The Diversity of Debt Crisis in Europe*', 202, http://www.cato.org/doc-download/sites/cato.org/files/serials/files/cato-journal/2011/5/cj31n2-2.pdf

debt crisis, with the prospect of those responsible for it coming up with another wondrous 'solution' that will only increase their power, the aim here is to show that there is a genuine solution, that will on the contrary, destroy the power that the money-lenders have exercised for centuries. The solution moreover, has been tried before and it has worked, on both small and large scales. It is a solution that is more from the 'Right' than from the 'Left', although non-dogmatic, non-Marxist Leftists such as John A Lee recognised the urgency of the demands. Moreover, what is demanded by such changes in the banking system is not – like Marxism and other forms of the Left – based on the smashing of tradition and millennia of cultural legacy – but, to the contrary, on the restoration of tradition. It does not demand the 'abolition of private property', as per Karl Marx, but results in the wider distribution of property among all classes, freed from the burden of mortgages and other crippling debt.

Financial reform is a natural, organic means of getting out of the increasing slavery of debt-bondage. It releases creativity, freedom, and inventiveness, while Marxism and Capitalism alike crush these human qualities, in the name of 'equality' under Marxism, and in the name of 'Market Forces' and 'efficiency' under Capitalism. There is a third way, which is not 'new' (or 'old') but which is eternally relevant, as the organic laws that govern economy are merely premised on the logic that currency and credit are intended as a convenient means of exchanging goods and services, and should always remain a mere token rather than become a profit-making commodity.

The Empire of Mammon

But they that will be rich fall into a temptation and a snare, and into many and hurtful lusts, which drown men in destruction and perdition. For the love of mammon is the root of all evil...
I Timothy 6: 9-10.

'The City' – or, 'The Square Mile' - refers to the *City of London Corporation*, a sovereign state like the Vatican. Together with Wall Street, The City forms the hub of the plutocratic system that controls most of the world, and is presently engulfing the few remaining states that it does not control, through the time-proven tactics of plutocracy: revolution ostensibly in the name of 'the people'.[1] Because 'The City' is situated in England, and because it is often confused with the ancient capital, London, there has been a lot of obfuscation as to the character of the plutocratic system that is partially based in The City. Hence, there has been a great deal stated, even by the well-informed, in regard to the British Empire and even the British Crown, being intrinsically a part of this international oligarchy. This is to misunderstand the nature of international capital, which owes no steadfast loyalty to any system of government, head of state, religion, ethos, nation, ethnicity or culture. Any such allegiance is conditional.

What is 'The City'?

The City of London Corporation is described in its promotional statements as 'the world's leading financial centre', and as 'the financial and commercial heart of Britain, the "Square Mile".[2]

---

1   K R Bolton, *Revolution from Above* (London: Arktos Media Ltd., 2011).

2   City of London , 'What is the City of London?', http://www.cityoflondon.gov.uk/

The City of London is at the heart of the world's financial markets. It is a unique concentration of international expertise and capital, with a supportive legal and regulatory system, an advanced communications and information technology infrastructure and an unrivalled concentration of professional services...[3]

The City of London Corporation is neither synonymous with Britain nor British interests, other than when these happen to coincide with the interests of international finance. That is why, although the British Empire has been defunct for over half a century, worn out by two world wars that did not benefit her a jot, and scuttled when empires became too restrictive for international finance, The City remains, in the words of its promoters, 'at the heart of the world's financial markets'.

Hence while Britain and the Commonwealth have a symbolic Head of State in the Monarch, the analogous Head-of-State for The City has precedence over the British Sovereign. The Lord Mayor of the City of London Corporation is 'not the Mayor of (Greater) London'; nor is he a 'mayor' in the limited sense of the word. He assumes the position as Head-of-State, not of merely a borough or a county. This Lord Mayor is elected for one year, and acts as a global ambassador for the international financial institutions situated in The City, and is 'treated overseas as a Cabinet level Minister'.[4] He lives in the palatial 250-year-old 'Mansion House'. On state visits the British Monarch waits at the Gate of The City to seek permission to enter and is presented with the sword of The City by the Lord Mayor.[5]

Corporation/LGNL_Services/Council_and_democracy/Council_departments/whatis. htm

3   Ibid., 'Business', http://www.cityoflondon.gov.uk/Corporation/LGNL_Services/ Business/

4   Ibid., *The Lord Mayor of the City of London*', http://www.cityoflondon.gov.uk/ Corporation/LGNL_Services/Council_and_democracy/Councillors_democracy_and_ elections/The_Lord_Mayor/

5   *History of Temple Bar*', http://www.thetemplebar.info/history

Dividend day at the Bank. London antique print c1880

This tradition has been preserved for more than 400 years, and the ceremony now is carried out on major state occasions where the Queen halts at Temple Bar to request permission to enter the City of London and is offered the Lord Mayor's Sword of State as a sign of loyalty.[6]

No matter how one rationalises the ceremony as an ostensible mark of 'loyalty' by The City towards the British Monarch, it is nonetheless the Monarch who is placed in a subordinated position in seeking permission for entry and waiting for a symbolic affirmation of loyalty from The City on each occasion.

International Finance

It should be kept in mind that 'international finance' is exactly that: international, not Dutch, German, British, or American. Jewish bankers might be loyal to Judaism or to Israel, and the French Huguenots who went to London had a religious identity, but international finance is not bound to the states of its residence. The 'modern' financial system did not originate in Britain, or even in the Occident. Ezra Pound, the famous poet who was also an avid opponent of usury-banking and an advocate of Social

6   Ibid.

Credit banking reform, traced the 'modern' usurious financial system back to 'the loans of seed-corn in Babylon in the third millennium BC'.[7]

From Holland to England

As indicated above, international finance can shift focus over the world as the requirements of commerce dictate. As for the shift of the Money Power to England, this can be traced to the English Civil War, and further back to the Reformation, where a Cromwell was significant in both. Thomas Cromwell, Secretary of State, who 'represented the mercantile community',[8] as distinct from the traditional rural interests, urged Henry VIII to suppress the religious Orders in 1533, Brooks Adams stating of this in his historical masterpiece, *The Law of Civilisation and Decay*, that:

> In 1533 Henry's position was desperate. He confronted not only the pope and the emperor, but all that remained of the old feudal society, and all that survived of the decaying imaginative age. Nothing could resist this combination save the rising power of centralized capital, and Henry therefore had to become the mouthpiece of the men who gave expression to this force. He needed money, and money in abundance, and Cromwell rose to a practical dictatorship because he was fittest to provide it.[9]

Adams details that the era of Henry VIII and the Reformation was the beginning of the speculative, capitalistic system. Additionally, 'The sixteenth-century landlords were a type quite distinct from the ancient feudal gentry. As a class they were gifted with the economic, and not with the martial instinct, and they throve on competition'.

---

7   Ezra Pound (1944) America, Roosevelt & the Causes of the Present War (London: Peter Russell, 1951), 6.

8   Brooks Adams, *The Law of Civilisation* (London: MacMillan, 1896), 230.

9   Ibid., 233.

The expansion of commerce in the wake of the Age of Exploration, and the formation of the British East India Company in 1600, five years after the East India Company in Holland, were symptoms of this historical trend that had already been set in motion by the Reformation. The merchant interests felt constrained by the Monarchy and another Cromwell, Oliver came forward, like his great-great-great-great-grand-uncle Thomas, to radically change England in the interests of money. The British Empire was expanding towards Asia and buccaneering was establishing fortunes.

> As the city grew rich it chafed at the slow movement of the aristocracy, who, timid and peaceful, cramped it by closing the channels through which it reached the property of foreigners; and, just when the yeomanry were exasperated by rising rents, London began to glow with that energy which, when given vent, was destined to subdue so large a portion of the world. Perhaps it is not going too far to say that, even from the organization of the East India Company, the mercantile interest controlled England. Not that it could then rule alone, it lacked the power to do so for nearly a hundred years to come; but, after 1600, its weight turned the scale on which side soever thrown.

> Macaulay has very aptly observed that but for the hostility of The City, Charles the First would never have been vanquished, and that, without the help of The City, Charles the Second could scarcely have been restored.[10]

The great English conservative philosopher Anthony Ludovici, commented on the forces arraigned against each other in the English Civil War:

> …and it is not astonishing therefore that when the time of the Great Rebellion[11] the first great national division

---

10   Ibid., 292-293.

11   The Cromwellian Revolution.

occurred, on a great political issue, the Tory-Rural-Agricultural party should have found itself arrayed in the protection and defence of the Crown, against the Whig-Urban-Commercial Trading party. True, Tory and Whig, as the designation of the two leading parties in the state, were not yet known; but in the two sides that fought about the person of the King, the temperament and aims of these parties were already plainly discernible.

Charles I, as I have pointed out, was probably the first Tory, and the greatest Conservative. He believed in securing the personal freedom and happiness of the people. He protected the people not only against the rapacity of their employers in trade and manufacture, but also against oppression of the mighty and the great...[12]

The Puritan Revolution was the first of the great revolutions undertaken in the name of 'the people' but in the interests of money interests. Such revolutions include the supposedly most anti-capitalist of them all, the 1917 Russian Bolshevik Revolution, and the wave of 'colour revolutions' that have swept through the former Soviet bloc, and most recently North Africa, again, all in the name of 'the people', but in the interests of big money.[13]

From the middle of the 16th Century capital accumulated, and 'the men adapted to be its instruments grew to be the governing class'.[14] Adams states of the era, 'In 1688, when the momentum of England suddenly increased, the change was equivalent to the conquest of the island by a new race'.[15] London became the centre of this global expansionist acquisition, a new Rome, where the wealth of the world was deposited:

12   A Ludovici, *A Defence of Conservatism* (1927), Chapter 3, 'Conservatism in Practice'.

13   K R Bolton, *Revolution from Above*, op. cit.

14   Brooks Adams, op. cit., 294.

15   Ibid., 298.

These hoards, the savings of millions of human beings for centuries, the English seized and took to London, as the Romans had taken the spoil of Greece and Pontus to Italy. What the value of the treasure was, no man can estimate, but it must have been many millions of pounds — a vast sum in proportion to the stock of the precious metals then owned by Europeans.[16]

What Adams calls a regime of merchants ruled England from 1688 to 1815. The wealth they accumulated, states Adams, became the primary source of power, and it was in the hands of a new breed of merchant: the bankers. 'With the advent of the bankers, a profound change came over civilization, for contraction began'.[17] The value of money as distinct from the mercantile concern at the value of wares was the concern of the bankers. At the close of the 18th Century 'the great hoards of London' passed into the hands of the bankers, the 'most conspicuous example' being the Rothschilds.[18]

It is here that we see a dichotomy arising between the old merchant, including the mercantile adventurers, such as Robert Clive of India, down to Cecil Rhodes, and on the other hand, the merchant bankers epitomised by the Rothschilds. It is here where the two are often mistaken as forming a common power elite.

Dr Carroll Quigley[19] described the character of international finance and the move of its centre to The City: 'Financially, England had discovered the secret of credit. Economically, England had embarked on the Industrial Revolution'.[20] Here we

---

16   Ibid., 305.

17   Ibid., 321.

18   Ibid., 321.

19   Carroll Quigley, of Harvard University, and the Foreign Service School at Georgetown University, was a scholar of considerable reputation, until he wrote a few dozen pages on the conspiratorial nature of international finance – albeit in a sympathetic light – in his 1300 page magnum opus *Tragedy & Hope* in 1966.

20   Carroll Quigley, *Tragedy & Hope* (New York: Macmillan Co., 1966), 48.

discern immediately a dichotomy operating within British power-politics: that of usury-based finance, which is cosmopolitan and parasitic, and that of the ingenuity of the Englishman and Scott as inventor and entrepreneur, as creator. It was this creativity and inventiveness, coupled with the bravery of the British military and the dedication of the British administrator, that was pressed into the service of parasitic finance, behind the cover of the British flag and Crown. These two factors at work: one cosmopolitan and one British, are often confused as being one and the same. Quigley continues:

> Credit had been known to the Italians and the Netherlanders long before it became one of the instruments of English world supremacy. Nevertheless, the founding of the Bank of England by William Paterson and his friends in 1694 is one of the great dates in world history.[21]

Quigley explained, far more succinctly than the professional economists, that the basis of the debt finance system is 'fractional reserves'. This method had its origin in the realisation by goldsmiths that they did not need to hold the equivalent of gold reserves in their vaults to the amount of paper certificates issued representing the value of gold. As there was unlikely to be a run on the vault by its depositors all demanding at once the return of their gold deposits, the goldsmith could issue paper certificates far in excess of the value of the amount of gold in his vaults.[22]

This fractional reserve remains the method of international finance; albeit no longer with the need for gold reserves. In particular, it should be kept in mind that the basis of the system is *usury*, where interest is charged for the loan of this bogus credit. Not only must the principal be paid back in real wealth – productive labour or creativity – but added interest.

Quigley remarks that 'in effect, this creation of paper claims

---

21   Ibid., 48.

22   Ibid., 48.

greater than the reserves available means that bankers were creating money out of nothing'. According to Quigley, William Paterson, having obtained the Royal Charter for the Bank of England in 1694 remarked, 'The Bank hath benefit of interest on all moneys which it creates out of nothing'.[23]

The centre of gravity for the merchant bankers had long been Amsterdam. The 'Republic of the United Provinces', which included Holland, had from the start accorded Jews, as the catalysts of incipient international free trade, equal protection.[24] According to Dr Stanley Chapman, Professor of Economic History at Nottingham University, the Sephardic Jewish community in Amsterdam had become adroit as lenders to foreign governments.[25]

Shall we, then, say that there had been a 'conspiracy of *Dutch* merchants to rule the world'? I think not. Yet neither can it be said in justice that this was a 'Jewish conspiracy' per se, although there are powerful Jewish elements that have their own agendas. The establishment of the Bank of England was a Protestant affair with anti-Catholic underpinnings. From France came the Huguenots who, like the Dutch Sephardic Jews, had established international connections through family networks across Europe and had also formed a community in The City, by the mid 18th century.[26] The English Revolution of 1642-1648, which established the republican Commonwealth under Oliver Cromwell in 1649, enduring under his son Richard until 1659, had opened the way for a shift of international banking from Amsterdam to London. There was impetus for British imperial expansion under Cromwell. The merchant coterie of

---

23 Ibid., 49.

24 *The Estates General of the Republic of the United Provinces: Declaration Protecting the Interests of Jews Residing in Holland',* 13 July 1657; in Paul R Mendes-Flohr and Jehuda Reinharz (ed) *The Jew in the Modern World: A Documentary History* (New York: Oxford University Press, 1980), 16.

25 Stanley Chapman, *The Rise of Merchant Banking* (Oxon: Routledge, 2006) 2.

26 Ibid., 4.

Amsterdam, which had backed Cromwell, was permitted entry into England. Menasseh ben Israel had appealed to Cromwell on the grounds of mercantile profitability to any nation that gave the Jewish merchant bankers freedom, as Amsterdam had done. The Jewish character of merchant banking at its embryonic stage cannot be denied, and can be accounted for by the nomadic type of existence the Jews were obliged to lead, whatever the reasons that might be said for this. Menasseh stated to Cromwell that profit was the best reason why the merchant bankers should be permitted into England:

> Profit is a most powerful motive, and which all the World prefers before all other things: and therefore we shall handle that point first. It is a thing confirmed, the merchandizing is, as it were, the proper profession of the Nation of Jews...[27]

Menasseh proceeded with explanations as to why this is so, due to the lack of opportunity from the time of the Exile, to possess a state of their own and to till the land, leading Jews to 'give themselves wholly unto merchandising' [sic]. Their dispersion throughout the world enabled them to form networks across borders, and to engage in commerce, with a common language that transcended the linguistic barriers of others.[28] Hence, these Jewish bankers acted as a cosmopolitan and internationalising tendency in commerce that we today call 'globalisation'.

The largesse for Cromwell's revolt against the British Crown had been provided by Antonio Fernandez Carvajal. His agents on the Continent also provided Cromwell with valuable intelligence. Carvajal had become wealthy through commerce on the Canary Islands, and in 1635 he settled in London. In 1649 he was one

---

27 Menasseh ben Israel, *'How Profitable the Nation of the Jews Are'*, 'to His Highness the Lord Protector of the Commonwealth of England, Scotland and Ireland', in Paul R Mendes-Flohr and Jehuda Reinharz, op. cit.,9.

28 Ibid., p. 10. The editors remark that although Menasseh's mission to Cromwell in 1655 was 'ostensibly unsuccessful, it did prepare the way for the resettlement of the Jews in England'. (Ibid., p. 12 Note 1).

of five merchants given the contract to supply Cromwell's New Model Army with corn, and continued to prosper under the Puritan Commonwealth, with a fleet of ships plying trade with the East and West Indies, Brazil and the Levant. He was both a financier to Parliament, and provided intelligence on English Royalists in Holland, and their relations with Charles II, to Cromwell through his agents.[29] While the supremacy of Money in England was set in motion by Henry VIII's Reformation, and the English Revolution a century later heralded the triumph of the merchant, it was not until the usurpation of the Throne by William III of Orange in 1688, with the deposing of James II, that the Bank of England was established. From then on a National Debt was owed to the usurers.

From the time of King Henry I *tally sticks* had served as the King's currency. These *tally sticks* were carved sticks broken lengthwise. The Chancellor of the Exchequer kept one half, and the King spent the other half into circulation,[30] like President John F Kennedy did in 1963, when he issued $4 billion 'United State Notes' directly into circulation via the US Treasury, circumventing the Federal Reserve Bank.[31] Eventually, the two halves would be matched to prevent counterfeiting. The *tally sticks* could be used as exchange for commerce and in payment of taxes. They circulated in England for 726 years until eliminated on the demand of the Bank of England in 1826.[32]

Although William was the maternal grandson of Charles I, he was born in Holland and destined to fulfil the legacy of Cromwell in placing England under the bondage of the merchant bankers, then centred in Holland. The anti-Catholic sentiment that had started under Henry VIII was a catalyst in assuring William

---

29 'Carvajal, Antonio Fernandez', *Jewish Encyclopedia*, 1906, www.jewishencyclopedia. com/articles/4089-carvajal-antonio-fernandez

30 L LaBorde, *'The Unholy Alliance'*, Silver Trading Company, Article #18, 12 February 2012, www.silvertrading.net/articles_metals_18_the_unholy_alliance.html

31 J F Kennedy, 'Executive Order 11110', 4 June 1963.

32 L LaBorde, op. cit.

support in driving James II from the Throne. Under William the authority of the Monarchy was reduced, and that of Parliament enhanced. The epochal act of William was to grant the Royal Charter to William Paterson to establish the Bank of England. This acquiescence might be explained by William having 'heavily borrowed in Amsterdam to fight his continental wars'.[33] The link between the bankers of Amsterdam and of London was maintained into the 19th century, and by the mid 18th century there was a considerable colony formed in the City by the scions of the Amsterdam banking families.[34]

The idea for the Bank of England came from the example of the Wisselbank, founded in 1609 which, according to the Bank of England's account, was the lender to the City of Amsterdam, the Province of Holland and the Dutch East India Company, exercising a monopoly over state borrowing and coinage.[35] The move to establish such a bank in England gained momentum 'after the Glorious Revolution of 1688 when William of Orange and Queen Mary jointly ascended the throne of England'. The political economist Sir William Petty wrote that the power of England would be magnified if there were a bank to lend the Throne credit.[36] He did not explain why it could not be a state bank issuing its own credit, and had to be a private bank accruing interest on credit that it makes out of nothing, as its founder, William Paterson, had boasted. According to Petty such a bank would 'furnish Stock enough to drive the Trade of the whole Commercial World'.[37] The Bank of England explains that after the rejection by Parliament of several proposals the bank and a 'Fund for Perpetual Interest' were accepted, having gained support from The City on recommendation by Michael Godfrey, 'a leading merchant'.[38]

---

33   Stanley Chapman op. cit. 2.

34   Stanley Chapman, ibid., 3.

35   '*Major Developments*', Bank of England, www.bankofengland.co.uk/about/history/major_developments.htm

36   Ibid., www.bankofengland.co.uk/about/history/major_developments.htm#2

37   Ibid.

38   Ibid., www.bankofengland.co.uk/about/history/major_developments.htm#2

In 1734 the Bank of England moved into a vast purpose-built building, nicknamed 'The Old Lady of Threadneedle Street', in The City.[39]

It was from the founding of the Bank of England that 'the funded National Debt was born'.[40] The present-day description of credit by the Bank of England is quite illuminating. The Bank's historical account states that at the time credit was called 'imaginary money'. Until then 'the man in the street' had simply thought of money as coins, but this 'shibboleth' was now overturned. Money could take other forms 'that had no intrinsic value'. 'The 18th century was a period dominated by governmental demand on the Bank for finance: the National Debt grew from £12 million in 1700 to £850 million by 1815, the year of Napoleon's defeat at Waterloo'.[41]

In 1946 the Bank was 'nationalised', but as in the nationalisation of other such banks, this means little, as the real authority comes from the creation of credit by the international merchant bankers. However, as the Bank's account states, in 1997 the Government formally handed its financial authorities over to the Bank and it 'thus rejoined the ranks of the world's "independent" central banks.'[42]

The purpose of these 'central banks', which the general public believes are controlled by governments, was to bring into their 'financial network the provincial banking centres… to form all of these into a single financial system on an international scale which manipulated the quantity and flow of money so that they were able to influence, if not control, governments on one side and industries on the other. The men who did this… aspired to

---

39 'Visit The City: the Bank of England', www.visitthecity.co.uk/index.php/attractions/ view/448/

40 Ibid., www.bankofengland.co.uk/about/history/major_developments.htm#2

41 Ibid., www.bankofengland.co.uk/about/history/major_developments.htm#3

42 Ibid., www.bankofengland.co.uk/about/history/major_developments.htm#5

establish dynasties of international bankers...[43] The centre of the system was in London, with major offshoots in New York and Paris, and it has left, as its greatest achievement, an integrated banking system...' [44]

---

43   Carroll Quigley, op. cit., 51.

44   Carroll Quigley, ibid., 50.

Rothschilds: Lords of International Finance

From the establishment of the Rothschild banking dynasty in England by Nathan M Rothschild, The City becomes synonymous with that dynasty. Further still, these suddenly 'British' Rothschilds become 'British' imperialists in the manner a chameleon changes his colour according to survival needs. It is the insinuation of the Rothschilds into the British power-structure that has generated much discussion on a 'British' imperial conspiracy centred around Cecil Rhodes and Alfred Milner, and the so-called 'Round Table Group' that they founded to extend British influence throughout the world. It is also frequently claimed that from this emerged an 'Anglo-American' conspiratorial 'network' that continues to the present in attempting to establish 'Anglo-American' global hegemony. Theorists of this 'Anglo-American network' most frequently cite Harvard historian Dr Carroll Quigley, who had access to what were presumably the papers of the Council on Foreign Relations, the self-described 'foreign policy Establishment' of the USA set up for the purpose of establishing a world government in the aftermath of World War I by international bankers.[1] For reasons not known to this writer, Dr Quigley, informative on so much in the course of his magnum opus, *Tragedy & Hope*, erred in thinking that an oligarchic 'Anglo-American network' was formed in the aftermath of World War I and continues to the present. We shall briefly examine this error in due course. However, for the moment Quigley had some pertinent things to say about both the Rothschilds and the 'international system of control' that was developing.

---

1   K R Bolton, *Revolution from Above*, op. cit., 30-32.

Portrait of Nathan M Rothschild

Quigley stated that one of the primary reasons the centre of international finance shifted to London was because the British upper class, which was not as rooted in noble birth as in money, 'was quite willing to recruit both money and ability from lower levels of society and even from outside the country, welcoming American heiresses and central-European Jews to its ranks'. This allowed the power structure to take on a cosmopolitan flavour.

Quigley described the development of the financial network by the international bankers into a world control system, and the assumption of the Rothschild dynasty to primacy:

In time they brought into their financial network the provisional banking centers, organized as commercial banks and savings banks, as well as insurance companies, to form all of these into a single financial system on an international scale which manipulated the quantity and flow of money so that they were able to influence, if not control, governments on one side and industries on the other. The men who did this... aspired to establish dynasties of international bankers and were at least as successful at this as were many of the dynastic political rulers...The greatest of these dynasties, of course, were the descendents of Meyer Amschel Rothschild… whose male descendants, for at least two generations, generally married first cousins or even nieces. Rothschild's five sons, established at branches in Vienna, London, Naples, and Paris, as well as Frankfort, cooperated together in ways which other international banking dynasties copied but rarely excelled.[2]

Quigley pointed out that these bankers were 'cosmopolitan and international rather than nationalistic',[3] and this, by the very nature of their business, is what they remain.

Brooks Adams states that towards the close of the 18th century the boards of The City passed from the merchants to merchant bankers, 'the most conspicuous example [being] the family of Rothschild'.[4] Adams writes of this dynasty:

In one of the mean and dirty houses of the Jewish quarter of Frankfort, Mayer Amschel was born in the year 1743. The house was numbered 152 in the Judengasse, but was better known as the house of the Red Shield, and gave its name to the Amschel family. Mayer was educated by his parents for a rabbi; but, judging himself better fitted for finance, he entered the service of a Hanoverian banker, named Oppenheim, and remained with him until he had saved enough to set up for himself. Then for some years he dealt in old coins, curiosities and bullion, married in 1770, returned to Frankfort, established himself in the house of the Red Shield, and rapidly advanced toward opulence. Soon after he gave up his trade in curiosities, confining himself to banking, and his great step in life was made when he became 'Court Jew' to the Landgrave of Hesse. By 1804 he was already so prosperous that he contracted with the Danish Government for a loan of four

2   Carroll Quigley, op. cit., 51.

3   Ibid., 51-52.

4   Brooks Adams, op. cit., 322.

millions of thalers. Mayer had five sons, to whom he left his business and his wealth. In 1812 he died, and, as he lay upon his death-bed, his last words were, 'You will soon be rich among the richest, and the world will belong to you'. His prophecy came true. These five sons conceived and executed an original and daring scheme. While the eldest remained at Frankfort, and conducted the parent house, the four others migrated to four different capitals, Naples, Vienna, Paris, and London, and, acting continually in consort, they succeeded in obtaining a control over the money market of Europe, as unprecedented as it was lucrative to themselves.[5]

Mayer Amschel had established his fortune by handling the financial affairs of William IX of Hesse-Kassel, who had been paid well by the British Government for supplying troops against the American revolt. At the time Amsterdam had been the capital of international banking, but the Napoleonic invasion of Holland had led to the closing of the Amsterdam Bourse, 'the leading Continental exchange'. Mayer Amschel and several others were situated to provide William IX with funds.[6] Additionally, in 1800 Mayer Amschel had become Imperial Crown Agent for the Emperor of Austria. He was what biographer Derek Wilson described as 'one of the first of a new breed of businessmen – the truly international merchant banker'. Wilson states that for centuries the Jews had played a prominent part in 'long distance commerce' due to their communal loyalty with which they were able to create a 'commercial sub-culture'. However, they were reliant on the patronage of rulers. Now, the revolutionary tumult in Europe had swept away traditional rulers and placed money on a footing of power. That is the nature of the bogus revolutions in the name of 'the people', whether that of Cromwell's revolt, the Russian revolts or the Jacobins in France. Each time, when the Monarch stood as the protector between his people and the

---

5   Ibid., 322-323.

6   D Wilson, Rothschild: *A Story of Wealth & Power* (London: André Deutsch Ltd., 1988), 17.

greed of the few, revolts were funded to commit regicide, in the name of 'liberty': liberty for economic exploitation on the ruins of thrones and altars.

War Against Napoleon

In 1798 Nathan Rothschild had set up shop in England and in 1806 he became a 'naturalised Englishman'.[7] The Rothschilds were backing the coalition against Napoleon, who was upsetting the Continental system of finance. In 1808 Nathan took over the financial affairs of the Landgrave William IX in England. That year he moved his business to 12 Great Helen's Street, The City, under the name of N M Rothschild and Brothers.[8] With agents throughout Europe, the Rothschilds were valuable allies in organising smugglers and couriers in the war against Napoleon. By now, on the initiative of Nathan Rothschild, 'the nerve centre of Rothschild operations had shifted from Frankfurt to London'.[9] Wilson reiterates that through Nathan's family and his 'large network of agents and couriers he was better informed about European affairs than any man in London – including members of the government'.[10] Wilson is altogether too charitable in ascribing 'patriotic' – British – motives to Nathan, in contrast to what he frankly says about the lack of national 'patriotism' among the other Rothschild brothers toward anything other than 'loyalty and responsibility to the Chosen People'.[11] Rather, Nathan and the rest of the dynasty were assisting in the fight against Napoleon because the upstart was undermining the financial system.

Brooks Adams described Nathan's character, the antithesis of the English noble, showing the nature of what was long derided as the vulgarity of 'new wealth', drawing on contemporary accounts:

---

7   Ibid., 21.

8   Ibid., 33.

9   Ibid., 34.

10   Ibid., 41.

11   Ibid., 42.

Of the five brothers, the third, Nathan, had commanding ability. In 1798 he settled in London, married in 1806 the daughter of one of the wealthiest of the English Jews, and by 1815 had become the despot of the Stock Exchange; 'peers and princes of the blood sat at his table, clergymen and laymen bowed before him'. He had no tastes, either literary, social, or artistic; 'in his manners and address he seemed to delight in displaying his thorough disregard of all the courtesies and amenities of civilized life; and when asked about the future of his children he said, "I wish them to give mind, soul, and heart, and body — everything to business. That is the way to be happy". Extremely ostentatious, though without delicacy or appreciation, his mansions were crowded with works of art, and the most gorgeous appointments. His benevolence was capricious; to quote his own words, 'Sometimes to amuse myself I give a beggar a guinea. He thinks it is a mistake, and for fear I shall find it out off he runs as hard as he can. I advise you to give a beggar a guinea sometimes. It is very amusing'.[12]

Such is the manner of those who think they are destined to govern the world by virtue of 'superior' qualities, 'superior' in all instances meaning wealthy rather than noble, intelligent or cultured. They are what the old landed aristocracy, themselves driven off the land through debt, after a long process of confiscation begun by Henry VIII, derided as the vulgarity of the 'new rich'. The traditional concept of *'noblesse oblige'* felt by the old landed aristocracy towards their people was replaced by a Rothschild amusing himself by flicking a coin to a beggar. The difference in attitudes remains to the present day.

Quigley explains that the credit creation mechanism that had been developed by the international bankers, as previously described, was to become one of the chief weapons in the victory over Napoleon in 1815. 'The emperor, as the last great mercantilist, could not see money in any but concrete terms,

---

12   Brooks Adams, op. cit., 323.

The Plumb-pudding in danger; or State Epicures taking un Petit Souper

and was convinced that his efforts to fight wars on the basis of "sound money", by avoiding the creation of credit [i.e. debt], would ultimately win him a victory by bankrupting England'.[13] Hence, the war against Napoleon was in part a war between two systems of economics involving the reorganisation of Europe.

Napoleon ended and reversed the madness of the French Revolution when he overthrew the Directory in November 1799. One historian of Napoleon states that, 'the bankruptcy of the Government had been the immediate cause of the French Revolution, and the Revolutionaries despite trying numerous experiments, failed to solve the government's fiscal problems'.[14] As acute observers of history and politics should by now realise, as in subsequent revolutions, under the French revolutionary regime, the merchant class remained in control,[15] behind the communistic façade of 'liberty, equality, and fraternity'[16]. The French Revolutionary government had tried circulating

---

13   C Quigley, op.cit., 49.

14   Robert B Holtman, *The Napoleonic Revolution* (New York: J B Lippincott Co., 1967), 20.

15   Ibid., 21.

16   The slogan of the French Revolution.

worthless paper money that they would not accept as payment for taxes, thereby undermining their own fiscal system, and paid 3 to 4% interest per month on debt.[17]

Napoleon established a stable currency standard, recognising the 'importance of state credit'.[18] France lacked a state bank from which industry and commerce could obtain credit. The Bank of France charter was approved in January 1800.[19] Although the bank had private bond holders, nobody could have more than five votes, regardless of the number of shares owned. Dividends were limited to 6%, after which the rest had to be invested in government bonds. In 1806 the bank was subjected to government control, and Napoleon decided who would become directors. The government decided when dividends were paid. Interest rates on loans were kept low, and therefore a banking plutocracy did not form.

The free market economics of the 'revolutionaries' was repudiated by Napoleon, and he subjected economics to state policy. Prices were fixed, rather than being left, as previously, to 'market forces'. The idea of corporations or guilds was revived for some trades despite opposition from commercial interests.[20] Economic self-sufficiency (autarchy) was the aim of France and her territories. The Government assumed control of all foreign trade, and tariffs protected certain French industries such as textiles.[21] When French industry faced a crisis in 1806-07 state loans of 6,000,000 francs were advanced to manufacturers at 2%.[22] Conciliation and arbitration boards to settle industrial disputes were first established in Napoleonic France decades before this 'modern' system of industrial relations was established elsewhere.[23] In these and other respects Napoleon was a

---

17   Holtman, op. cit., 103.

18   Ibid.

19   Ibid.

20   Ibid., 106.

21   Ibid., 112.

22   Ibid., 114.

23   Ibid., 118.

precursor of the Fascist and Catholic corporatist regimes (Dollfuss' Austria, Salazar's Portugal) over a century later. He sought an autarchic France and ultimately an autarchic Europe that would not be subjected to the dictates of plutocracy. Hence, he was fought by the same economic and financial interests that declared war on Germany, Japan and Italy around 140 years later.

The British Empire & Cecil Rhodes

It is a significant error of interpretation for otherwise sound historians such as Carroll Quigley or E C Knuth,[24] to suppose that there is an 'Anglo-American' – network working for world rule. It is also erroneous to assume that because the merchant bankers found it opportune to lend credit to Governments that ruled over empires, these bankers, who are cosmopolitan, have an enduring commitment to some type of nationally or racially based imperialism, whether it be British, German, Dutch, Spanish, Belgian or Portuguese, etc. These empires were scuttled when the centre of gravity for international finance moved to New York following World War II, and the old imperial systems of trade had become obstacles to global free trade. As President Franklin D Roosevelt reminded Winston Churchill, who felt that the post-war world the USA was about the create would destroy the British Empire:

'Of course, after the war, one of the preconditions of any lasting peace will have to be the greatest possible freedom of trade. No artificial barriers....' Roosevelt stated that imperial trade agreements would have to go, and remarked that the Third Reich's incursion into European trade had been a major cause of the war.[25]

This theory of an 'Anglo-American' network written of by Quigley had been adopted by conspiracy theorists such as W

24   E C Knuth (1946), *The Empire of 'The City'*, Milwaukee, Wisconsin; reprinted 1982 (no other publication details).

25   Elliott Roosevelt, *As He Saw It* (New York: Duell, Sloan and Pearce, 1946), 35.

Cecil John Rhodes founder of the diamond company De Beers,
and the African territory of Rhodesia.

Cleon Skousen.[26] The basis of these theories centres on Lord
Rothschild being the banker to Cecil Rhodes. The theory states
that Lord Natty Rothschild was part of Rhodes' secret society,
the Round Table Groups, that aimed to spread the benevolence
of British imperialism over the world.[27] These imperial ideals
were said to be motivated by the teachings of the Oxford art
historian John Ruskin, who exhorted his students to take British
culture to the ends of the Earth.

While Lord Rothschild saw the Empire as the means by which
commerce could be spread and maintained by force of arms, the
support was pragmatic, and owes nothing to a commitment to
any British ideals as envisaged by Rhodes et al. Derek Wilson
writes of this in relation to Lord Rothschild's opposition to
Gladstone's 'flabby' foreign policy: 'But Lord Rothschild was
not an unbridled expansionist. This is clearly shown by his
relationship with a man who **was** an unbridled expansionist

---

26   W Cleon Skousen, *The Naked Capitalist: A Review & Commentary on Dr Carroll
     Quigley's Book Tragedy & Hope* (Salt Lake City, Utah, 1971).

27   Carroll Quigley, op. cit., 131. W Cleon Skousen, op. cit., 30.

– Cecil Rhodes'.[28] When diamonds were discovered in South Africa, the Rothschilds bought into the Anglo-African Diamond Mining Company Ltd., which was amalgamated with DeBeers. In 1887 Rhodes returned from South Africa to Britain to ask Lord Rothschild for financial backing. Lord Rothschild saw this as the means of establishing commercial stability in South Africa against his main rival, the Barnato Diamond Mining Company, which also ended up merging with DeBeers.[29] For Rhodes making money was a means of spreading British imperial ideals. Not so for Rothschild, although Rhodes persuaded himself that Natty was of like mind. 'He was wrong. Lord Rothschild was not an unreserved imperialist, as Rhodes gradually discovered'. In 1888 Rhodes made a will nominating Natty to administer most of his estate for funding The Round Table Groups. Wilson writes:

> In response to Rhodes' suggestion that company funds be used to finance territorial expansion, his banker advised: 'if … you require money to finance territorial expansion, you will have to obtain it from other sources than the cash reserves of the DeBeers Company'. And Rhodes cannot have been very pleased to learn, in 1892, that Rothschilds had floated a loan for the Boer government of the Transvaal.[30]

The Rothschilds were interested in commercial stability, not British imperial expansion. By the time of the abortive Jameson Raid organised by Rhodes against the Boer Transvaal Republic in 1895, he had long ceased to have close and cordial relations with Natty. Probably he never grasped the fact that, though the Rothschilds disliked Gladstone's policy of colonial retrenchment, they were not advocates of unbridled imperialism for its own sake.[31] Hence, when a few decades later imperialism became a hindrance to unbridled international free trade, the international bankers used the newly

---

28   Derek Wilson, op. cit., 303.

29   Ibid., 304.

30   Ibid., 305.

31   Derek Wilson, ibid.

emergent power of the USA to scuttle the old European Empires over the course of half a century, and the oligarchs moved into the power-vacuum of the new decolonised states.[32]

This myth of the 'Anglo-American network' for world control is centred around a supposed alliance between the Royal Institute of International Affairs (RIIA) and the US globalist think tank, the Council on Foreign Relations (CFR), referred to previously. Again, this assumed alliance is erroneous: the proffered alliance between the two bodies never eventuated. Far from there being accord between supposed 'Anglophiles' on both sides of the Atlantic, there was a breach. Peter Grose, the CFR's historian, mentions that both sides rejected the suggested alliance before it eventuated.[33]

The Rothschilds were concerned with Britain's imperial links 'for sound commercial reasons', but with 'maximum freedom of trade'.[34] It was inevitable that 'free trade' and the old European imperialism were going to conflict. The role assumed by the USA in subverting and destroying the old empires can be discerned by 'The Fourteen Points' decreed by President Woodrow Wilson as the blueprint for the post-war world in 1918,[35] and by the 'Atlantic Charter',[36] imposed on Britain by President Roosevelt in 1945, both of which focus on international free trade as the basis for the world economy and which specifically repudiate the old empires.[37]

Soon after World War II the Rothschilds increased their focus

---

32   A K Chesterton, *The New Unhappy Lords* (Hampshire: Candour Publishing Co., 1975).

33   Peter Grose, *Continuing The Inquiry: The Council on Foreign Relations from 1921 to 1996*, (New York: Council on Foreign Relations, 2006). The entire book can be read online at: Council on Foreign Relations: www.cfr.org/about/history/cfr/index. html

34   Derek Wilson, op. cit., 305.

35   W Wilson, '*Fourteen Points*', 1918, www.fordham.edu/halsall/mod/1918wilson.html

36   Franklin D Roosevelt and Winston S. Churchill, 'The Atlantic Charter', 14 August 1941, www.usinfo.org/docs/democracy/53.htm

37   E Roosevelt, op. cit., 31, 35.

on Wall Street, and their hitherto relatively small Amsterdam Incorporated was reformed as an investment bank named New Court Securities, its share capital being taken up by the Rothschild banks in Paris and London. Where hitherto the Rothschilds had mainly been concerned with negotiating loans with states, they were now involved in the rapid post-war expansion of western commerce and industry, [38] freed up by the destruction of the old empires, and the inauguration of a new era of international financial agreements, formalised by the Bretton Woods Agreement.

This is what the biographer Wilson calls the Rothschilds' 'new, deliberate internationalism';[39] no longer constrained by nation-states and empires. However, 'The City' remains a focus. The Rothschilds led the way in forging links between Tokyo and London. Edmund co-led a delegation from 'The City' to Tokyo in 1962 and received The Order of the Sacred Treasure from Emperor Hirohito. Regardless of these new avenues opened up for post-war globalisation and free trade, certain plutocratic traditions remain features of 'The City': the 'Gold Fixing Room' at the Rothschild offices, New Court, continues to be the place where the leading London bullion dealers daily sit around a table 'to agree on the price of gold'. N M Rothschild 'continues to be the most important bullion dealer' in Britain.[40] Of the 'four hundred and eighty banks in the city', Rothschild remains supreme.[41]

---

38   Derek Wilson, op. cit., 397.

39   Ibid.

40   Ibid., 436.

41   Ibid.

The Global Debt-Finance System

The 'Inexorability of its own Negation'

Much of the world is undergoing a periodic debt crisis, with the panaceas demanded by the Left and by orthodox financial advisers (often misidentified as the 'Right') being those of expropriating private wealth, and 'austerity' respectively. Both measures are outmoded, ineffective and ultimately destructive. The system by which the financial and therefore the economic and social structures of most nations is predicated on is that of debt-finance. That system was designed for the benefit of what have been termed 'money creators',[1] but it is inherently flawed. While Marx said that capitalism contained the seeds of its own destruction, by ignorance or calculation, he wrongly identified the flaw in the system as private property, and advocated the abolition of private property instead of getting at the cause: the debt finance system functioning through usury. Even the Soviet bloc imploded partly through a mountain of debt to the international banks.

It is the nature of parasites that they eventually destroy their hosts and either move to another host or self-destruct. The financial system, under which much of the world operates, is by nature parasitic and therefore not only destructive but self-destructive. It was Marx who said that capitalism contains the seeds of its own destruction: 'Capitalist production begets with the inexorability of a law of nature its own negation. It is the negation of negation'[2] But it can be said with more accuracy that

---

1   Gertrude M Coogan, *Money Creators* (Sound Money Press, Chicago, 1935).

2   K Marx, 'Historical Tendency of Capitalist Accumulation,' in *Das Kapital*, Vol. I, Chapter 32, 1867, www.marxists.org/archive/marx/works/1867-c1/ch32.htm

the debt-finance system contains the seeds of its own destruction. Since it is fundamentally parasitic it cannot do anything but turn upon itself when the host has been bled white. While attention was focused on Greece in the present debt crisis, what was not so widely perceived is that Britain, Spain, and Ireland are more indebted than the Hellenes, and a time of reckoning is 'inexorably' approaching.

The present debt crisis has exposed the banking system for all who have eyes to see, but not to solutions which would entail replacing the debt-system altogether. Although attention was focused by the US Senate on an international financial icon, Goldman Sachs (which moreover is a world power player and one of the major backers of Obama's presidential campaign, as was Lehman Brothers[3]), among the finger-pointing and accusations, the politicians will not advocate anything beyond closer state scrutiny or regulations involving the finance sector; when it is the system itself that requires changing. This debt crisis is not so much the result of a conspiratorial mechanism as it is the result of a parasitic mechanism. It was after all the need for an orderly financial system and regulation that the international bankers themselves had the US Senate inaugurate the Federal Reserve Bank System in the USA in 1913. Paul Warburg of the international banking dynasty was the architect of the US Federal Reserve Bank Act. Such central banks, including New Zealand's Reserve Bank, the Bank of England, and others of the type, gave the public the impression that banking would be subjected to the state in the public interest. Yet this was not the case. Even when these banks became nationalised and the state bought out the private bondholders, as in New Zealand, these central banks have continued to operate within the debt-finance system or what we might refer to as *usury*.

Goldman Sachs has been 'grilled' by a Senate committee for a year. Senator Claire McCaskill (Democrat, Missouri) put it

---

3   K R Bolton, 'Obama: Catspaw of International Finance,' 28 August 2008. www.rense. com/general83/cats.htm

to Goldman Sachs representatives: 'You are the bookie, you are the house. You had less oversight than a pit boss in Las Vegas'.[4] Goldman Sachs' influence behind the scenes on the global political stage and their financial patronage for Obama have not saved the company from public scrutiny. What might however turn out to be a 'conspiratorial' outcome to this crisis is whether these same bankers whose system is responsible for the crisis, are able to foist upon the world one of their own 'solutions' to problems of their system's own making, as is often the case. Any 'solution' to the global financial crisis is likely to involve more power being concentrated into the hands of the International Monetary Fund, thereby strengthening the very system responsible for the crisis.

Parasitism

The debt finance system is parasitic in the sense of taking without returning anything positive to the host. The host is the nation-state, the individual, the family, the businessman, the farmer, the community, and the world.

While there are entire disciplines and professions devoted to explaining economics, the manner by which the financial system operates and the way in which its inherent flaws can be eliminated is comparatively straight-forward, but seldom explained.

Fundamental Question

The fundamental question is: If a private bank can create and lend credit as a profit-making commodity by charging interest, then why can't a government create its own credit as a public service and purely as a means of exchange of goods and services without incurring debt through exorbitant interest?

---

4   J Shenn and M J Moore, 'Goldman Sachs Executives Grilled in Senate Hearing', *Bloomberg Businessweek*, July,2010, www.businessweek.com/news/2010-04-27/ goldman-sachs-grilled-in-senate-hearing-over-mortgage-business.html

Credit and currency are only supposed to be a convenient method of commerce, instead of exchanging a bag of potatoes for a sack of flour, etc. It is because credit has become a prerogative of private banks, instead of governments acting on behalf of the people, that the interest incurred on credit loaned as debt sucks real money, created from actual production, out of circulation, and enables it to be re-lent by the money-lenders at interest, and so the process continues, with debt accruing all the while, with financial booms and busts. There is never enough purchasing power for the consumer to buy the full value of production. One result is export wars which can conclude in shooting wars. Moreover, interest *compounds* because loans must be taken out at interest to repay the interest on previous loans. The result is eventually a credit bust where the banks, operating through the International Monetary Fund, foreclose not simply on individuals and businesses but on entire nations, and stringent 'austerity measures' are placed on the hapless citizens, while the state is forced to sell off the nation's assets to pay off the debt. One example of this was that the debt accrued from New Zealand's 'Think Big' projects that were supposed to lessen New Zealand's dependency on overseas energy resources, had to be sold off to repay the interest on the loans that had to be raised to pay for the projects. New Zealand's National Debt similarly began with public works for national development inaugurated by Treasurer Julius Vogel[5] who borrowed from the London Rothschilds[6]

Harvard historian Carroll Quigley included in his magnum opus *Tragedy and Hope*, which served as the basis for his university lectures, a history of the banking system that is particularly cogent. Quigley traced the mechanism of present-day banking to the founding of the Bank of England in the 17th century:

The founding of the Bank of England by William Paterson

---

5   Julius Vogel, 'Budget Speech, 28th June 1870', in W D McIntyre and W J Gardner (eds.) *Speeches and Documents on New Zealand History* (Oxford: Clarendon Press, 1971), 43-51.

6   A N Field, *All these Things* (Hawthorne, California: Omni Publications, 1963), 219.

and his friends in 1694 is one of the great dates in history... It early became clear that gold need be held on hand only to a fraction of the certificates likely to be presented for payment... In effect the creation of paper claims greater than the reserves available means that bankers were creating money out of nothing. The same thing could be done in another way. Deposit bankers discovered that orders and cheques drawn against deposits by depositors and given to a third person were often not cashed by the latter but were deposited in their own accounts. Accordingly it was necessary for the bankers to keep on hand in actual money no more than a fraction of deposits likely to be drawn upon and cashed, the rest could be used for loans, and if these loans were made by creating a deposit (account) for the borrower, who in turn would draw cheques upon it rather than withdraw money, such 'created deposits' or loans could also be covered adequately by retaining reserves to only a fraction of their value. Such created deposits were also a creation of money out of nothing... William Patterson however, on obtaining the Charter of the Bank of England in 1694, said: 'the bank hath benefit of interest on all moneys which it creates out of nothing'[7]

Few states have been able to remain outside this system of international finance. Even Vietnam, having fought for centuries for unity and sovereignty, is part of the IMF debt web. The World Bank states of Vietnam: 'The level of public debt, at 42 % of Gross Domestic Product, is moderate and is considered to be sustainable'.

Banks and bankers are looked upon virtually as wizards and shaman who alone can conjure up 'money' or more accurately *credit*, since most commerce is undertaken through credit rather than currency. For example, New Zealand has a mere $3 billion in Reserve Bank notes and coins in circulation. Of this the banks only hold half a billion NZ Dollars on deposit. However the total

---

7   C Quigley, *Tragedy and Hope*, op. cit., 48-49.

of all New Zealand bank deposits is $200 billion. The difference between the $200 billion in bank deposits and the half billion in bank cash is the amount of credit the banks have created out of nothing. New Zealand banks no longer even have to operate on a 'fractional reserve.' They can create credit at will.[8] Banks thereby reap huge profits in interest by creating credit that did not hitherto exist. This situation is the foundation of banking throughout the world.

There is deliberate obfuscation on the nature of money and credit creation, since the professional economists are taught at such institutions as the London School of Economics, which was endowed by financiers including Sir Ernest Cassel, and the Rothschild and Rockefeller dynasties. The fact of Cassel having established the chair of 'economic geography'; and of Sir Evelyn Robert de Rothschild having been a Governor of the London School of Economics attests to the influence of the international bankers on such institutions that instruct our economists, who then obtain positions with governments and corporations throughout the world.

However during the 1920s and 1930s people in general understood much more about the way the financial system operates than they do today. They simply did not trust bankers or economists.

In 1924 The Rt. Hon Reginald McKenna, who had been Chancellor of the Exchequer, stated to shareholders of the Midland Bank in Britain, of which he was then chairman:

> I am afraid the ordinary citizen will not like that the banks can, and do, create money... and they who control the credit of a nation, direct the policy of governments, and hold in the hollow of their hands the destiny of the people.[9]

---

8   I Sheen, *The Truth About Money*, (Figures from the NZ Reserve Bank (Otaki, New Zealand, 2008), 1.

9   R McKenna, Midland Bank Report, England, January 1924.

In 1955 a Royal Commission was convened in New Zealand to study the 'monetary, banking and credit system' concluding that: 'the fact that a large proportion of our money supply comes into existence as a result of the operations of the trading banks obviously disturbed many witnesses.'[10]

Worldwide Awakening During the Great Depression

When the Great Depression hit there were enough independent thinkers about to examine the flaws in the financial system and propose solutions, and enough desperate people to want to seek out and understand the answers and then to demand their implementation. Not so today where mass apathy and ignorance reign, and our political leaders and their advisers and media tell the common people that the world is now much too 'complex' to return to such 'simple' solutions. Yet the financial system today is the same as it was when its parasitic nature caused the Great Depression.

Congressman Louis T McFadden, who had for ten years served as Chairman of the Congressional Banking and Currency Committee, and had been a banker himself, was particularly active in exposing the nature of the Federal Reserve System and the operations of the debt-finance system in speeches before Congress. In 1932 McFadden stated in the House:

> Chairman, we have in this Country one of the most corrupt institutions the world has ever known. I refer to the Federal Reserve Board and the Federal Reserve Banks, hereinafter called the Fed. The Fed has cheated the Government of these United States and the people of the United States out of enough money to pay the Nation's debt. The depredations and iniquities of the Fed has cost enough money to pay the National Debt several times over.

---

10   *Report of the New Zealand Royal Commission on Monetary, Banking and Credit Systems* (Wellington: Government Printing Office, 1956), 164.

Illusion and reality - unemployment line Chicago 1937

This evil institution has impoverished and ruined the people of these United States, has bankrupted itself, and has practically bankrupted our Government. It has done this through the defects of the law under which it operates, through the maladministration of that law by the Fed and through the corrupt practices of the moneyed vultures who control it.

Some people think that the Federal Reserve Banks are United States Government institutions. But they are private monopolies which prey upon the people of these United States for the benefit of themselves and their foreign customers; foreign and domestic speculators and swindlers; and rich and predatory money lenders. In that dark crew of financial pirates there are those who would cut a man's throat to get a dollar out of his pocket; there are those who send money into states to buy votes to control our legislatures; there are those who maintain International propaganda for the purpose of deceiving us into granting of new concessions which will permit them to cover up their past misdeeds and set again in motion their gigantic train of crime.[11]

11   Louis T McFadden, United States Congressional Record, 10 June 1932.

McFadden reminded Congress that the Federal Reserve Bank had been inaugurated by the introduction in 1913 of the Federal Reserve Act by Senator Aldrich, and the Act had been drafted primarily by Paul Warburg of Kuhn, Loeb and Co. McFadden held the Great Depression to be the responsibility of the Federal Reserve, which was not a 'state bank' owned by the people, but was owned by private shareholders, and still is. The Great Depression was caused when the Federal Reserve recalled its loans from the network of 12 provincial Federal Reserve Banks via which the entire US banking system operated; the ordinary bank customer was obliged to repay his debt or face foreclosure. McFadden said of the system:

> Meanwhile and on account of it, we ourselves are in the midst of the greatest depression we have ever known. From the Atlantic to the Pacific, our Country has been ravaged and laid waste by the evil practices of the Fed and the interests which control them. At no time in our history, has the general welfare of the people been at a lower level or the minds of the people so full of despair.[12]

Poverty Amidst Plenty

It is the parasitic nature of the debt-finance banking system that causes the criminal phenomenon of 'poverty amidst plenty'. This was most dramatically illustrated in the Western world within living memory during the Great Depression. People do not suddenly became lazy and refuse to work, to produce, to grow crops or raise livestock. Yet because of the lack of purchasing power – money and credit – caused by the trading banks having to recall their loans due to the dictates of the New York Federal Reserve Bank, there was not sufficient purchasing power to consume production. The most graphic example of this was the state imposed demand that farmers destroy their crops and livestock, while masses of people were starving, because the purchasing power was not available to buy the produce. In

---

12   Ibid.

Starvation in the midst of plenty. The Irish "Potato Famine" of 1845-51

short, people starved, while food was destroyed. Farmers took their families and simply walked away from their land because they could not afford to repay the interest on their mortgages to the banks.

This system of banking is no less brutal than the mass starvation that was caused in the Ukraine by the confiscation of grain. The power of the Federal Reserve, i.e. the private bankers who own, and continue to own the bonds, was explained by McFadden:

> …In defiance of this and all other warnings, the proponents of the Fed created the 12 private credit corporations and gave them an absolute monopoly of the currency of these United States; not of the Fed Notes alone but of all other currency![13]

Another infamous example is the 'Irish Potato Famine' of the 19th Century. Mass starvation resulted in over a million deaths in a country of about 8,000,000. Yet the only crop that had failed was that of potatoes. In 1845 Ireland exported 779,000 quarters of wheat and flour, 93,000 quarters of barley, and 2,353,000

---

13   Ibid.

quarters of oats; enough to feed for a year every person who died of starvation, four times over. Exports had to be maintained to repay Ireland's creditors. The money-lenders took precedence over feeding people.[14]

---

14   H J Kelliher, *New Zealand at the Cross-Roads,* (Auckland, New Zealand, 1936), 147. Kelliher, later knighted, was a director of the Bank of New Zealand, chairman of Dominion Breweries, and proprietor of *The Mirror.*

Breaking the Bondage of Interest

Money is merely the medium of trade. It is not wealth.
It is only the transportation system, as it were, by which
wealth is carried from one person to another.
Father Charles Coughlin (1935)

It is historically ironic that at the very time the world groans under the inexorable self-negation of the debt-finance system, nothing is offered by the Right as an alternative. Hilariously, the mighty USA is threatened with default on debt amounting to trillions of dollars. States across the world, from Greece to New Zealand are broke. Their debt is so mountainous it is no longer sustainable. The only answers – offered by those who have maintained the debt system – are to 'tighten your belts' with 'austerity measures', sell off assets to global corporations, themselves a part of the international debt finance system – and establish a new world banking system that will empower the usurers more than ever.

The reaction of masses of people is reaching violent proportions. Individuals and families cannot 'tighten their belts' until they are impoverished, while nothing is done to deal with those responsible for their plight. There is rioting in Greece and elsewhere. The rioting seems to be invariably led by the Left; especially with black masked anarchists in the forefront. Yet the Left has offered nothing at all other than the usual banality about 'soaking the rich', which at best would result in equality of impoverishment rather than assisting the masses of people an iota.

Where is the Right?

But where is the Right with leadership and alternatives? The Right seems to be invisible on issues affecting the inevitable results of the debt-finance system. Where financial matters are examined the policies put forward are as absurd as those of the Left: lower taxes, return to the gold standard, audit the Federal Reserve. None of this amounts to anything. The once impressive Social Credit movement, formulated by Maj. C H Douglas during the 1920s and 1930s, squabbles dogmatically over technicalities. Hence, Social Credit in New Zealand, for example, which several decades ago took 25% of the vote, is all but unknown.

While focusing on immigration, Jews, holocaust revisionism, etc. the Right in general, and worldwide, now seems for the large part oblivious to the very crucial issue of finance and banking. The banking system is the mechanism by which world control is exercised by the financial elites. Whether Jewish or Gentile, the system is the same and it is largely a moot point to argue about who invented it if one isn't even aware of what to do about it.

Any party of the Right that does not include banking reform as a major plank in its platform is neither 'Right' nor of any relevance. This was widely realised among the Right until the 1970s or so, and George Knupffer, the Russian Monarchist émigré, in his proposals for a 'Party of the Right', regardless of the country, focused on this as the most crucial of issues, as will be seen below. Hence, back in 1958, the National Labour Party (NLP) in Britain, one of the precursors of the modern British Rightist movement, had among its seven core principles: 'A sound financial system should be based on the nation's ability to produce goods; not on the power of the banks to create paper debts at will'.

It was a Conservative Member of Parliament, Captain Henry Kirby, who in the post-war years was among the most determined opponents of usury, moved before Parliament in 1964:

The continued issue of all the means of exchange—be they coin, bank notes or credit largely passed on by cheque—by private firms as an interest-bearing debt against the public should cease forthwith; that the Sovereign power and duty of issuing money should be returned to the Crown, then be put into circulation free of all debt and interest obligations, as a public service, not as a private opportunity for profit and control for no tangible returns to the British people... so as to assure the State and Nation the benefits of that emission and relieve them of the immense and growing burdens of a parasitical National and private debt; and to make certain that control passes to the taxed and is taken out of the hands of the present hidden unlawful beneficiaries of taxation ... this House calls upon Her Majesty's Government to introduce the required legislation... to assure unprecedented prosperity with true sovereignty and liberty.[1]

No other policy of the Right, in whatever part of the world, is possible without the need to first secure the economic and financial sovereignty of the state, and this can only be achieved when the State or the Crown assume the prerogative over banking and credit creation. The bottom line is that no State - and hence people - are truly free while any decisions that are made can be undermined and wrecked by decisions made in the Boardrooms of global corporations, by the fluctuations of the world Stock Market, and by the power of bankers to turn off the credit supply if a state pursues policies not in the interests of plutocracy. Furthermore, no political party can guarantee the welfare of the people – including party promises of 'full employment' - when the State or Crown does not control the economic lifeblood of a nation: credit. All other issues, including the Right's now usually be-all issue of race and immigration, are secondary, and no Rightist government could implement Rightist policies until the sovereignty of credit creation is achieved.

---

1   Captain Henry Kirby, MP, House of Commons, 22 December 1964.

The great issue of our time – that of driving out the money-lenders - has not changed, but the understanding of both the masses of people and the Right that was once the custodian of this struggle, has changed, like much else in the modern era… for the worse. It is time, more than ever, amidst the breakdown of the debt system, for the Right to reclaim its role as leader in the fight for Social Justice against usury.

Fortunately, the British Democratic Party, newly formed as this is written, attempting to reinvigorate and reunite a fragmented Right, does include in its founding policy platform the necessary formula for both social justice and national sovereignty, stating:

> Macro-economic policy must be based on the principle that *what is physically possible must be financially possible, otherwise there is something wrong with the financial system.* This means that if there are unemployed workers and unsatisfied needs that they could fulfil, the financial system must facilitate the satisfaction of those needs.

> The current financial system is one in which much of the money supply is created by private banks on the basis of the banks' need to make a profit, rather than the needs of the economy. The quantity and form of money in circulation must be under the control of the Bank of England, which must be independent of the government of the day.[2]

It is a policy that should be espoused to the forefront of all else, despite its relegation to a humble position behind other policies. As I have attempted to show throughout, the problem of banking, currency and credit over-rides all others, and no policy, whether on national sovereignty, immigration, race relations, housing, or law and order, can be resolved until this is first addressed. Even from the viewpoint of practical politics, with massive

---

2   Policy Statement of the British Democratic Party: 'Economic Policy', www.nationalistunityforum.co.uk/index.php/policy-statement-of-the-british-democratic-party/

unemployment, and the pervasive phenomenon of debt, from the usury charged on an individual's credit card, to the bankruptcy of an entire nation due to debt, a campaign for the 'breaking of the bondage of debt' has the potential to create an upsurge of popular support for the party that can simply and forcefully espouse it. Without taking a partisan view of party-politics, especially in a nation other than my own, the British Democratic Party seems to have been the only party to re-discover a once widely recognised fundamental truth. Perhaps others will follow.

Movements for Banking Reform

As one would hope, the methods of credit and banking were major issues of the Depression Era. Our grandparents were acutely aware of such matters. They were discussed in factories, offices, pubs and homes. Now few among even the well informed are aware of the issues. Yet banking reform was more an issue of the Right than the Left, the latter hedging their bets on the 'nationalization of the means of production', or on graduated income tax, and banking reformers on the Left such as New Zealand's John A Lee or Australia's King O'Malley fought uphill against the leadership of their own Labour parties. As even hard-line communist states have shown, nationalization of industry, and even an internal credit system operating through state banks, does not necessarily extricate one from the international banking system, as witnessed by the mountain of debt that was incurred by the USSR. Even Vietnam is part of the World Bank, and has embarked on a policy of privatisation, which it euphemistically (or dialectically?) calls a 'socialist-oriented market economy'.[3]

When economic crisis hit the world during the 1920s, unlike today there was no shortage of programmes and movements advocating realistic solutions. Significant impetus came in the English-speaking world from the Scottish engineer Maj. C H

---

3   K R Bolton, 'Has Vietnam Lost the Struggle for Freedom?' *Foreign Policy Journal,* June 10 2010, www.foreignpolicyjournal.com/2010/06/10/has-vietnam-lost-the-struggle-for-freedom/all/1

Douglas who formulated Social Credit. This doctrine calls for the issuing of credit according to sound accounting principles, based on the productivity of a nation. Douglas wrote his seminal Social Credit book *Economic Democracy* in 1919, followed by *Credit-Power and Democracy* (1920), *The Control and Distribution of Production* (1922), *Social Credit* (1924), and *The Monopoly of Credit* (1931), among others. Interestingly, he had discerned the nature of the problem prior to the Great Depression. In 1933 he established, as an educational institute, the Social Credit Secretariat, which still exists.[4] The fundamental premise remains: 'Money is not Wealth but only its token, and tokens cost next to nothing to produce. So what is physically possible and socially desirable can certainly be made financially possible'.[5]

Green Shirts of England

In Depression Era Britain Social Credit assumed a refreshingly militant form with the Green Shirts for Social Credit, led by John Hargrave. Readers might recall the enigmatic dedication in Ezra Pound's booklet *Social Credit: An Impact*, to 'the Green Shirts of England'.[6] Hargrave had led a woodcraft youth movement emerging from the Boy Scouts movement, called Kibbo Kift, from archaic Kentish, meaning 'a proof of great strength'. Like the Wandervogel in Germany, it had folkish interests which harked back to Medievalism and the Saxon heritage. Folk moots and Althings were organized, and the movement's units were called Clans and Tribes. The movement had support from the Fabian socialists, but at the 1924 Althing a socialist faction attempted to take over and was expelled by Hargrave.

Hargrave met C H Douglas in 1923 and recognised Social Credit as the means of purging civilisation of corruption just as his woodcraft movement helped the individual with that aim.

---

4   Social Credit Secretariat, www.douglassocialcredit.com/

5   Ibid.

6   E Pound, *Social Credit: An Impact, 1935*; reprinted by Peter Russell, London, 1951.

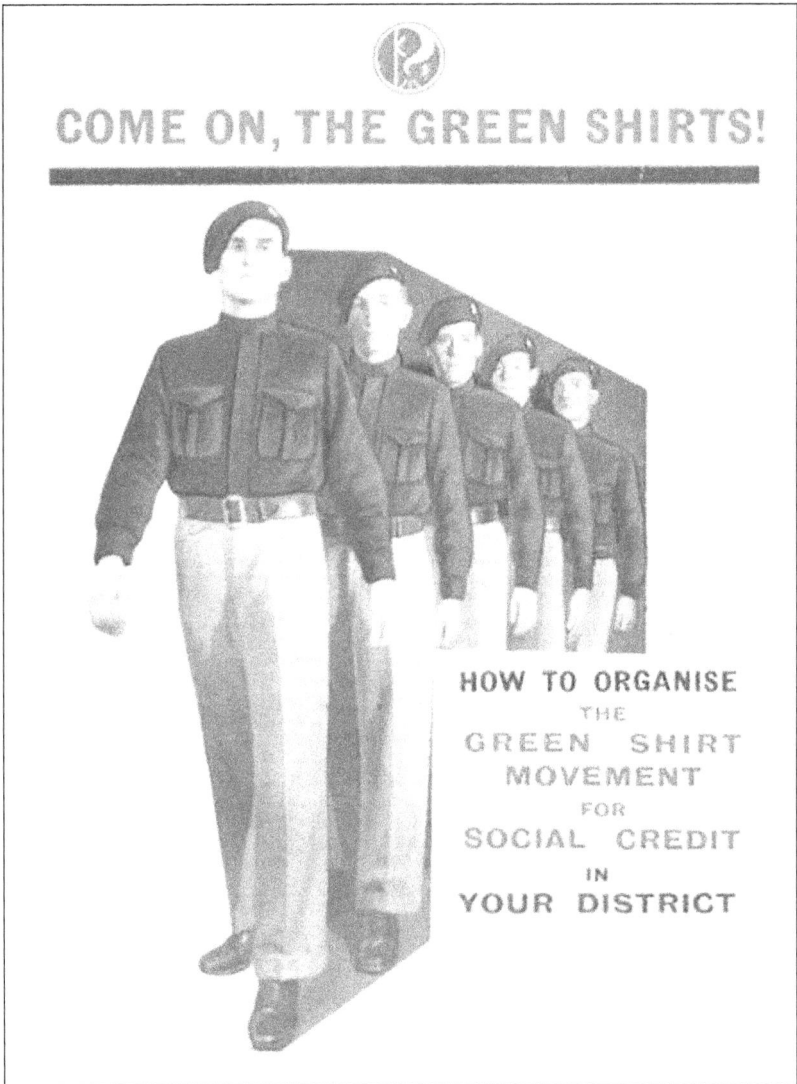

COME ON, THE GREEN SHIRTS!

HOW TO ORGANISE THE GREEN SHIRT MOVEMENT FOR SOCIAL CREDIT IN YOUR DISTRICT

Hargrave stated: 'Half our problem is psychological and the other half economic. The psychological complex of industrial mankind can only be released by solving the economic impasse'. By 1927 Hargrave had converted most of the leadership of Kibbo Kift to Social Credit and he was able to add a Social Credit plank to the movement's principles. In 1930 a Legion of the Unemployed was establish in Coventry, which adopted a paramilitary style green shirt and beret. Soon the Legion was affiliated with Kibbo Kift and in 1932 the woodsmen adopted the green shirt and changed their name to the Green Shirt Movement for Social Credit.

In 1932 Hargrave had stated at the Althing that breaking the power of the 'money mongers' could not be done through parliament but only through a movement that was based on 'that absolute, that religious, that military devotion to duty without which no great cause was ever brought to a successful issue'. Hargrave advocated a militant campaign that would break the media blackout. The Green Shirts took to the streets on marches, behind drums and banners, held street corner meetings, and sold newspapers on the street, delivering the Social Credit message in a cogent manner. Facing the violent opposition of the Left, they were noted for their discipline in the face of provocation. They led hunger marches and demonstrations of the unemployed in thousands of open-air meetings and demonstrations. They were also noted for throwing green painted bricks through the windows of banks and using the consequent court cases to publicise their views.

In 1936 Hargrave was appointed economic adviser to the new Social Credit Government in Alberta, Canada, and drew up the 'Hargrave Plan'. Not surprisingly, Alberta was prevented from properly implementing the Social Credit policy due to the interference of the central government. A post-war campaign for Social Credit continued under the National Social Credit Evangel, along with the Social Credit Party. The movement eventually fizzled. In 1976 there was a stage musical about the Green Shirts and Hargrave was acclaimed when he attended the performance.[7]

---

7 K R Bolton, *John Hargrave & the Green Shirt Movement* (Paraparaumu Beach, New Zealand: Renaissance Press, 2003). K R Bolton, 'State Credit and Reconstruction: The First New Zealand Labour Government', *International Journal of Social Economics*, (London: Emerald Publishing Group) Vol. 3, No. 1, 2011.

New Zealand Legion

In New Zealand a conservative reaction to the Left formed around the New Zealand National Movement under Maj. J R V Sherston. The popular physician Campbell Begg soon assumed leadership, and the movement was renamed the New Zealand Legion. The movement reached 20,000 members and adopted a Green Shirt uniform. In 1934 C H Douglas undertook a lecture tour of New Zealand, which had significant results. Begg met Douglas twice,[8] and the New Zealand Legion adopted state credit as a means of securing social justice without recourse to socialism.

For a conservative reaction to socialism, comprised mainly of adherents from the middle class and veterans, albeit with support from the National Union of Unemployed Workers, the NZ Legion was the most genuinely radical movement in terms of its 'Begg Plan'. It was therefore opposed by orthodox elements of the Left which called the NZ Legion 'fascist' and a reactionary ploy of the bosses, and by the bogus 'Right' which was aghast at the Legion's radical platform. One of the 12 points of the Legion program was the 'control of currency by the state'.[9] Eventually the Legion was undermined from within, with a possibly predominant faction rejecting Begg's aim for the Legion to put up candidates for Parliament, while many were uneasy at the seemingly 'socialistic' policies or state interference. Begg withdrew from leadership and settled in South Africa. Those candidates for the Legion who stood in local body elections as Independents did well.

---

8   M C Pugh, *'The New Zealand Legion & Conservative Protest During the Great Depression'*, MA Thesis, (Auckland University, 1969), 128-129.

9   C Begg, 'The Legion's 12 Points', *National Opinion*, Wellington, New Zealand, Vol. 2, No. 14, 1934, 1.

Mosley's Fascism

Generic fascism incorporated opposition to the banking system whether from syndicalist or Catholic sources or a synthesis of these. Any genuine national sovereignty must be predicated on the nation's financial sovereignty, otherwise anything less is a fraud.

In 1938 Social Credit was advocated within Sir Oswald Mosley's British Union of Fascists on the premise that the British Union sought to end usury, and the Douglas method was the way to do it. W K A J Chambers-Hunter was able to appeal to the British Union policy that had already been formulated by Mosley in *Tomorrow We Live*. Mosley's type of British 'Fascism' began primarily as one of economics aiming to reject the international financial system, make the British Empire a self-sufficient trading bloc and change the mechanism of finance to ensure that the whole of production could be consumed. Mosley stated that a 'complete revolution in our financial system is required'. A Financial Corporation would be constituted to control all organs of finance and credit, on the premise that 'British credit shall be used for British purposes'.[10] Mosley wrote:

> Within such a system the supply of credit must be adequate to a system of greater production and greater consumption. The British credit system will rest on certain clear and basic principles:
>
> That British credit created by the British people shall be used for British purposes alone;
>
> That British credit shall be no monopoly in the hands of a few people, and often alien hands at that, but shall be held in high trusteeship for the British people as a whole;
>
> That British credit shall be consciously used to promote

---

10   Oswald Mosley, *Tomorrow We Live* (London: Greater Britain, 1938, 1939), 50.
       Available from the publisher, Black House Publishing.

Oswald Mosley addresses a British Union meeting. Earls Court, London, 1939

within Britain the maximum production and consumption by the British of British goods;

That the credit system shall maintain a stable price level against which the purchasing power of the people is progressively raised in the development of higher wages.[11]

Alexander Raven Thomson, Policy Director of the British Union of Fascists, who had been educated at the best universities of Scotland, Germany and England, in describing the money masters of Britain, pointed out that British Fascists were well aware that merely nationalising the Bank of England would not resolve the problem of the financial dictatorship exercised by the international bankers. He wrote that,

Nationalisation of the mere mechanism of the Bank [of England], such as advocated by the Labour Party, will be of as little avail as the recent nationalisation of the Bank

---

11   Ibid., p. 52.

of France by M Blum and the French Socialists, unless the 'distant control' over the Bank by finance houses and gold bullion brokers is also removed.[12]

Thomson's comments on the worthlessness of nationalising banks if they are only going to assume the function of state banks borrowing from private sources, continues to apply to the banking systems of most nations, but is little understood by the Left and is disregarded by much of what has become the misnamed 'Right'. Thomson stated that the policy of British Union would be to expand the home market by ensuring that the whole of production could be consumed by means of 'commodity currency' based not on gold or private credit creation charging interest (usury), but on the supply of money 'upon the production of useful goods and services offered for sale'. This would 'make money, not the master, but the servant of industry'.[13]

Fascists and Social Crediters both aimed to take control of the credit mechanism away from usurers and return it to the people. There are major differences, as the Social Crediters in particular will point out, in eagerness to distance themselves from Fascism. However, the aforementioned W K A J Chambers-Hunter was an adherent of both Social Credit and Mosleyite Fascism, as was the poet Ezra Pound.

Chambers-Hunter, British Union organizer and prospective parliamentary candidate for Aberdeen, pitched his advocacy for Social Credit within British Fascism by showing its relevance to the policy of 'British Credit' that had been explained by Mosley in *Tomorrow We Live*. Chambers-Hunter stated that when British Union assumed power the 'best brains' would be brought in to implement the details of Mosley's financial and economic program. One such expert would be C H Douglas, 'that honoured pioneer of new thought in this sphere'.

---

12   A Raven Thomson, *Our Financial Masters* (London: British Union of Fascists, 1937), 15.

13   Ibid., 16.

Poverty in the 1930's - London 'East End'

Chambers-Hunter wrote that, 'It is as a member of the British Union, and also as a believer in the essential truth of Major Douglas's theory, that I write this pamphlet'.[14]

There were some essential differences, however, including the perennial bugbears among Social Crediters as to whether the policy should be implemented by the state or by an independent credit authority, and the widespread suspicion of political parties of any type, including even Social Credit parties. However, Chambers-Hunter stated that 'it is not only possible to believe in Social Credit and to belong to the British Union; I go further and say that if we believe in Social Credit we must realise that only through British Union have we any hope of an executive instrument, through which a nation "free of Usury" can be built'. Chambers-Hunter was writing to explain 'proposals for the execution of British Union policy by Social Credit Method'.[15]

---

14   W K A J Chambers-Hunter, *British Union & Social Credit* (London: British Union of Fascists, 1938), 4.

15   Ibid., 4.

Certainly, one might be compelled to admit that given the forces arraigned against any state that attempts to free itself from usury, only a strong state of the Fascist type would have ability to oppose those forces.

A + B Theorem

Chambers-Hunter begins with a fundamental Douglas premise: the amount of money in circulation is never equal to the ability to consume the whole of production. This difference was explained by Douglas' A + B Theorem. 'A' equals the payments a producer makes to his employees; 'B' represents the payments he makes outside his business. Only 'A' is available as purchasing power, while 'B' payments are not spent on consumption in any given week. Therefore prices cannot be less than the costs to the producer of A + B, but the purchasing power to consume those goods is only reflected in 'A'. 'Therefore there is a shortage of purchasing power by the amount of the B payments'. For the consumption of production to be adequate 'there must be purchasing power equivalent to the "B" payments distributed from some other source'.[16] Social Credit advocates a 'National Dividend' to make up for any shortfall of purchasing power, given to every citizen as a shareholder as a birthright.

Chambers-Hunter explained the short-fall of the system in providing adequate finance for both production and consumption:

> At present the power of creating, and destroying credit, which performs over 95% of the function of money is actually excised by the financial system on its own and is quite independent of industry, agriculture, or any of the people's needs. Consumption, and consequently production are cut down to suit the purposes of this hidden power instead of the purposes of the people.[17]

---

16 Ibid., 5-6.

17 Ibid., 11.

Chambers-Hunter explains that to make up for this shortfall in consumer power, credit 'will be created by the State alone and will be issued as required as a right and not as a debt'. The state credit issued by banks at local level to farmers, fishermen, industrialists, etc., would carry a minimal fee, perhaps of half a percent, but would nonetheless be sufficient to cover the costs of issuing credit.[18]

What might be said in summary of all such theories is that credit would be issued as a public service to facilitate the exchange of goods and services, and not as a profit-making commodity.

Ezra Pound On Economics

As mentioned previously, another exponent of both Fascism and Social Credit was Ezra Pound. Pound wrote a series of booklets on banking and history that are especially lucid. These include *Social Credit: An Impact* (1935), *The Revolution Betrayed* (British Union Quarterly, 1938), *What is Money For?* (1939), *A Visiting Card* (Rome, 1942), *Gold & Work* (Rapallo, 1944), *An Introduction to the Economic Nature of the United States*, and *America, Roosevelt and the Causes of the Present War* (Venice, 1944). Also notable is his 'With Usura', part of the *Pisan Cantos*. The reader is going to get more cogency on economics and banking from the poet Ezra Pound than he is ever going to get by attending an economics class, or reading books by professional economists.

Pound met C H Douglas at an early stage (1917), with the guild-socialist A R Orage, who was a major influence in promoting both social reform and new literary talent, through his journals *The English Review* and *The New Age*.[19] Indeed, Orage is said to have coined the term 'Social Credit'.

Orage, although a leading Fabian-Socialist, was at loggerheads

---

18   Ibid.

19   K R Bolton, *Artists of the Right* (San Francisco: Counter-Currents Publishing, 2012), Chapter 8: 'Ezra Pound'.

Ezra Pound (1885 - 1972) American poet and critic.

with most other Fabians insofar as he believed that a new society and ownership should be based on a revival of the Medieval guilds rather than being based on the State. Pound considered Fascist Italy to be partially achieving Social Credit aims in breaking the power of the usurers over politics and culture, writing:

> This will not content the Douglasites nor do I believe that Douglas' credit proposals can permanently be refused or refuted, but given the possibilities of intelligence against prejudice in the year XI of the Fascist Era, what other government has got any further, or shows any corresponding interest in or care for the workers?"[20]

---

20 Ezra Pound, *Jefferson and/or Mussolini*, 1935 (New York: Liveright, 1970), 126.

In *Social Credit: An Impact*, Pound wrote of Fascism in relation to economic reform:

> Fascism has saved Italy, and saving Italy bids fair to save part of Europe, but outside Italy no one has seen any fascism, only the parodies and gross counterfeits. Douglas for seventeen years has been working to build a new England and enlighten England's ex- and still annexed colonies.[21]

Pound saw both Italy and Japan trying to throw off the system of usury, writing:

> Japan and Italy, the two really alert, active nations are both engaged in proving fragments of the Douglas analysis, and in putting bits of his scheme into practice...

> The foregoing does not mean that Italy has gone 'Social Credit'. And it does not mean that I want all Englishmen to eat macaroni and sing Neapolitan love songs. It does mean or ought to mean that Englishmen are just plain stupid to lag behind Italy, the western states of America and the British Dominions...[22]

Pound's *Canto XLV* ('With Usura'), written while he was confined to an animal cage in Italy after being arrested by the Americans at the end of World War II, is a particularly cogent exposition on how the usury system infects social and cultural bodies, and is analogous to the New Zealand poet and Social Credit advocate Rex Fairburn's *Dominion*.[23] Pound provides a note at the end defining usury as, 'a charge for the use of purchasing power, levied without regard to production: often even without regard to the possibilities of production'.

---

21   E Pound, *Social Credit: An Impact,* 1935; reprinted by Peter Russell, London, 1951, 7.

22   Ibid., 19.

23   K R Bolton, *Artists of the Right,* op. cit., Chapter 12, 'Rex Fairburn'.

With usura…
no picture is made to endure nor to live with
but it is made to sell and to sell quickly
with usura, sin against nature,
is thy bread ever more of stale rags
is thy bread dry as paper…
And no man can find site for his dwelling.
Stone cutter is kept from his stone
Weaver is kept from his loom
WITH USURA
Wool comes not to market
Sheep bring not gain with usura…
Usura rusteth the chisel
It rusteth the craft and the craftsman
It gnaweth the thread in the loom…
Usura slayeth the child in the womb
It stayeth the young man's courting
It hath brought palsey to bed, lyeth
Between the young bride and her bridegroom
CONTRA NATURAM
They have brought whores to Eleusis
Corpses are set to banquet
At behest of usura.[24]

'With Usura' precisely reflects Pound's position that the financial system denies the cultural heritage and creativity of the people, creates poverty amidst plenty, and fails to act as a mechanism for the exchange of the productive and cultural heritage. Creativity either fails to reach its destination or is stillborn. We might with this poem in particular understand why Pound felt the problem of banking and credit to be of crucial concern for artists.

Father Coughlin & Social Justice

One of the greatest movements against usury during the Depression was in the USA and centered on Father Charles Coughlin who, in alliance with Senator Huey Long, had the

---

24   *Ezra Pound: Selected Poems 1908-1959* (London: Faber & Faber, 1975), 'Canto XLV: With Usura', 147-148.

Father Charles Coughlin

potential to create a new America. That movement was aborted with the assassination of Long[25] and an order from the Church hierarchy that silenced Father Coughlin.

Coughlin had been an adviser to Roosevelt and thought the 'New Deal' would implement Catholic Social Doctrine, as developed in particular by Pope Leo XIII in his encyclical of 1891, *Rerum Novraum*.[26] Catholic Social Doctrine had laid the basis for many states and political movements that resisted the Money Power, from Dollfuss' Austria and Salazar's Portugal to Vargas' Brazil. Pope Leo's words inspired the creation of the anti-socialist and anti-capitalist 'Distributist' movement in England, headed by the Catholic literary figures Hilaire Belloc[27] and G K Chesterton.[28] And the Church's historic opposition to usury had prompted

25   G L K Smith, *Besieged Patriot*: Gerald L K Smith (Eureka Springs, Arkansas: Christian Nationalist Crusade, 1978),120-126.

26   Pope Leo XIII, *Rerum Novarum.* : Rights and Duties of Capital and Labour, 1891, www.vatican.va/holy_father/leo_xiii/encyclicals/documents/hf_l-xiii_enc_15051891_ rerum-novarum_en.html

27   T Southgate (ed.) *Belloc: Thoughts & Perspectives Volume XII* (London: Black Front Press, 2013).

28   T Southgate (ed.) *Chesterton: Thoughts & Perspectives Volume XIII* (London: Black Front Press, 2013).

many Catholics to support the Social Credit movement, one of the longest enduring and most effective continuing to be the Pilgrims of Saint Michael, discussed below.

Coughlin had started by broadcasting a children's' radio show for four years every Sunday from his Church of the Little Flower in Royal Oak, Michigan. But one broadcast on 30 October 1930 was addressed to the parents on the subject of the 'money changers'. Such was the immediate support that he organized his listeners into the Radio League of the Little Flower. Soon after his first broadcast denouncing usury Coughlin was receiving 50,000 letters a week. The broadcasts were extended via the CBS network, and had an estimated 10,000,000 listeners. He organised to assist the poor in Detroit, and in 1932 campaigned for Roosevelt under the slogan 'Roosevelt or Ruin'. By the time of the presidential race in 1932 he was reaching up to 45,000,000 listeners.[29] He was strongly supported by Bishop Michael Gallagher of Detroit. There is thought to have been a letter to Coughlin from Pope Pius XI thanking him for promoting the ideas of *Rerum Novarum*. However, Coughlin was also attracting powerful opposition and in 1933 CBS refused to renew his contract unless they were able to approve his sermons in

---

29   I Leighton (ed.) *The Aspirin Age* 1919-1941 (London: The Bodley Head, 1950), W Stegner, 'The Radio Priest & his Little Flock', 234-236. Stegner's chapter, as one would expect, is a mean-spirited polemic, but nonetheless informative, if read critically. For example Stegner incorrectly alludes to Coughlin's reference to an 'American Secret Service' report on the link between Jewish Communists and Jewish bankers as being a fraud and an invention of Nazi Germany's 'World Press Service'. Stegner also states that a reference to Jewish involvement in the Bolshevik revolution allegedly published in a British White Paper is false. In reality, the American Secret Service report exists and is entitled 'Judaism and Bolshevism', 13 November 1918, State Department Decimal File (861.00/5339). The report is cited by Dr Antony Sutton, *Wall Street & the Bolshevik Revolution* (New York: Arlington House, 1974), 186-187. Likewise the supposedly fraudulent passage on Jews and the Bolshevik Revolution in the British White Paper, although censored from a subsequent edition, appears in the original. The statement was from Oudendyk, Minister of The Netherlands in Petrograd, who was acting for British interests after the murder of Capt. Cromie by the Bolsheviks. A photostatic reproduction of the cover of the original White Paper is given by R Gostick, *The Architects Behind the World Communist Conspiracy* (Ontario: Canadian Intelligence Publications, 1968), ii. The White Paper is entitled *A Collection of Reports on Bolshevism in Russia* (London: His Majesty's Stationery Office, 1919) Russia No. 1 (1919). The passage in question is reprinted on page 5 of Gostick's book.

advance. Coughlin refused and created his own radio network.[30] In 1934 the Church of the Little Flower was extended into a considerable administration centre with a large staff. That year marked Coughlin's rejection of the 'New Deal' and his creation of the National Union for Social Justice.[31] But Coughlin now started receiving opposition from the Church hierarchy, at first from Cardinal O'Connell of Boston, whom Coughlin rebuffed as lacking jurisdiction.

The 16 Point Social Justice program was a cogent expression of Catholic Social Doctrine that upheld private property within the framework of economic and financial reform based on opposition to usury:

- Abolition of private banking, and the institution of a central government bank.

- The return to Congress of the right to coin and regulate money.

- Control of the cost of living and the value of money by the central government bank.[32]

In 1936 Coughlin founded the newspaper, *Social Justice*, which was sold on the streets by Irish lads contending with the violence of Jewish Communists, organised Jewry regarding Coughlin as 'anti-Semitic' for his opposition to usury, while the Communists saw in the 'Coughlinites' a mass movement that offered something better than Marxism or capitalism. In 1938, for self-defense, the *Social Justice* salesmen were organized into platoons of 25 under the banner of the Christian Front. However, with the death of Bishop Gallagher the way was open for the closing down of Coughlin through manoeuvres by the New Dealers and the Church hierarchy.

---

30   W Stegner, Ibid., 237.

31   Ibid., 239.

32   Ibid., 240-241.

By this time, 'there was hardly a section of even the Catholic press… which defended him'.[33] In October 1939, after the outbreak of war in Europe, the National Association of Broadcasters changed regulations and by April 1940 Coughlin's broadcasts were finished. As events heated up in Europe, the street fighting in the USA intensified. In 1942, after Pearl Harbor, *Social Justice* was banned from the mail by the US Post Office department.

Gerald Smith, former aide to the late Senator Long, a Protestant pastor and one of Coughlin's colleagues, relates that he was told by Coughlin that in seeking diplomatic relations with Washington the Pope had agreed to get Coughlin silenced on political matters. Smith remarks: 'From that time on Fr. Coughlin descended into a state of semi-retirement and frustration and I always had the feeling that he suffered from a broken heart'.[34]

Pilgrims of Saint Michael

However, one of the most zealous and longest-running organisations that continue to battle usury is a Catholic organization run from Canada, Coughlin's land of birth.

Louis Even, who had seen Social Credit as the means of implementing Catholic Social Doctrine, started the movement in Quebec in 1935. A French language journal was established in 1939. The English language newspaper *Michael* was founded in 1953, with subsequent editions in other languages, and the organization took the name Pilgrims of St Michael in 1961. Louis Even wrote of the crucial issue of finance:

> It is because every economic problem, and almost every political problem, is above all a money problem. We never say that the money question is the only one to be solved, or the only one that must be dealt with. We do not even say

---

33   Ibid., 251.

34   G L K Smith, op. cit., 71-72.

that it is the highest one, but it is certainly the most urgent one to solve, because all the other issues come up against this money problem.[35]

There is a wealth of material on the banking system on the movement's website. There is even a reprint from Fr Coughlin's *Money Questions & Answers*,[36] that Louis Even included as an appendix in his book, *This Age of Plenty*. The Pilgrims of St Michael continue with a crusading zeal seldom seen among Social Crediters since the 1930s.

Catholic Church Condemned Usury

The historic opposition of the Church prompted the rise of banking reform movements such as the above named Social Justice movement of Father Coughlin in the USA, and the Pilgrims of St. Michael based in Quebec. However, during the high point of Western culture - the Medieval era - prior to the Reformation that enthroned the money lenders, the usurers often subverted even the canonical laws.

Opposition to usury was fundamental to the Church's approach to society. The *Catholic Encyclopaedia* states that at first it was only prohibited for clerics to charge interest on loans:

> ... Nevertheless, the 12th canon of the First Council of Carthage (345) and the 36th canon of the Council of Aix (789) have declared it to be reprehensible even for laymen to make money by lending at interest. The canonical laws of the Middle Ages absolutely forbade the practice. ... and the Third of the Lateran (1179) and the Second of Lyons (1274) condemn usurers. In the Council of Vienne (1311) it was declared that if any person obstinately maintained that there was no sin in the practice of demanding interest,

---

35   'What is Michael?', www.michaeljournal.org/aboutus.htm

36   www.michaeljournal.org/appenC.htm

he should be punished as a heretic.[37]

However, the people often had to bypass princes, lords and even kings to appeal to the Pope for help against usury, as the political hierarchy was frequently indebted to usurers – that is to say, Jews at that time, because they were exempted from decrees against usury, thus causing much of the bitterness against them. In Portugal in 1353 after complaints about the ostentatious display of luxury by Jews the King issued a decree against usury whereby nobody could be forced to pay more than 33⅓%.[38] Considering that is a heavy 'reduction', the mind boggles as to what charges were being levied on loans. In France, Louis IX set the interest rate at 40%, a law that was nonetheless circumvented by money-lenders.[39] However under Jean II during the latter half of the 13th century the rate was raised to 80% and Jewish usurers enjoyed a privileged position. In 1388 Charles VII allowed the usurers to take not only 80% but compound interest, and it was forbidden to criticise the practices of the money-lenders.[40] The eminent Jewish writer Bernard Lazare, in examining the causes of anti-Semitism, stated:

> The Middle Ages considered gold and silver as tokens possessing imaginary value, varying at the will of the king, who could order its rate at the dictations of his fancy. This notion was derived from Roman law, which refused to treat money as a merchandise. The church inherited these financial dogmas, combined them with the biblical prescriptions which forbade loan on interest, and was severe from its very start, against the Christians and ecclesiastics even that followed the example of the *feneratores*, who advanced money at 24, 48 and even 60 per cent., when the legal rate of interests was 21 per cent.

---

37   'Usury', *Catholic Encyclopaedia, 1917*, www.newadvent.org/cathen/15235c.htm

38   Alfred Rosenberg, *The Track of the Jew Through the Ages* (East Sussex: Historical Review Press, 2012), 63-64.

39   Ibid., 78.

40   Ibid., 80.

The canons of councils are quite explicit on this point; they follow the teachings of the Fathers, Saint Augustin, Saint Chrysostom, Saint Jerome; they forbid loans and are harsh against those clerics and laymen who engage in the usurer's business.[41]

Note here, importantly, despite Lazare's disparaging tone, that even from Roman times gold and silver were regarded as tokens of exchange and not as commodities from which profit can be made, and the value was set by the king. Although the practice was often flawed, and even in Roman times that Civilisation was rife with money-lending by the patrician class as described in detail, by Brooks Adams,[42] it is descriptive of traditional attitudes toward money only as a means of exchange.

Lazare commented that kings would occasionally prohibit usury to give relief to their subjects and cancel debts, but 'oftenest they encouraged Jews, tolerated them…', and after banishment would soon come re-entry, as they were the best financiers and tax collectors. In particular, the monks, closest to the people and knowing their plight, preached against usurers, but were often stifled by the kings, princes and the Bishops.[43] Thus there was a continual flux in fortunes of the Jewish usurers during the Medieval era, and they were by no means always at the rough end of history, but on the contrary, their spiteful parades of wealth often caused tempers to boil among those who endured under the bondage of usury.

---

41   Bernard Lazare (1894), *Antisemitism: Its History and Causes* (London: Britons, 1967), 60.

42   Brooks Adams, *The Law of Civilisation & Decay* (1896), online: www.archive.org/details/lawcivilization00adamgoog

43   Bernard Lazare, op. cit., 66-67.

States that Broke the Bondage of Usury

Any efforts to advocate alternatives to banking that might extricate nations from the grip of the money-changers are dismissed as 'funny money' by defenders of a system that has for centuries resulted in 'poverty amidst plenty', cycles of economic bust and war, and servitude at every level. Yet there are many examples of states that have broken free and implemented alternative forms of banking that have brought well-being, while others have languished in stagnation at best while paying their hidden masters for the privilege via usury.

Of course it is not in the interest of the financial and economic status quo that any light be shed upon these historical examples, and they are put down the Memory Hole, or the nature of their financial systems is obscured by focusing entirely on other factors. Hence, while many financial reformers are aware of the way Lincoln funded his war partly through the issue of Greenbacks, few even among banking reformers realise that the Confederacy was also funded with state credit called Graybacks, and that system is obscured by focusing on questions of slavery. Likewise, few understand much about the manner by which Germany extricated itself from socioeconomic misery through a new financial system and the matter is buried by focusing on the Holocaust, war, or when there is an attempt to explain Germany's reconstruction it is ascribed to 'rearmament'.

It took a poet, Ezra Pound to explain more cogently about the history of money than economists and historians. Pound stated that:

The history of usury begins with the loans of seed-corn in

Babylon in the third millennium BC. The first mention I know of a state monetary policy refers to the year 1766 BC when an Emperor of China, in order to alleviate distress caused by famine and aggravated by grain monopolizers, opened a copper mine and coined discs of metal perforated with a square hole. We read that he gave this money to the starving, and that they could then buy grain where the grain was.[1]

Nearly four thousand years later and the politicians either did not have the wisdom or the courage to adopt a similar policy for getting food on the table of the starving during the Great Depression, or for dealing with the present global debt crisis without getting into further debt or implementing 'austerity measures'.

Pound wrote of the Medici bank, the Monte di Paschi, that had been founded in 1600 and remained standing in his own time: 'Siena was flat on her back, without money after the Florentine conquest'. Cosimo, first Duke of Tuscany, guaranteed the capital of the bank, using grazing lands as collateral. He underwrote 200,000 ducats, paying 5% to shareholders and lending at 5½%, with minimum overheads and salaries, and profits going back into hospitals and public works.[2]

Of the American Colonies Pound wrote that, 'The Colony of Pennsylvania lent its colonial paper money to the farmers, to be repaid in annual instalments of ten percent, and the prosperity that resulted was renowned throughout the western world'.[3] He wrote that in 1750 there were sanctions imposed by the Bank of England forbidding Pennsylvania from issuing its own 'scrip', which played its role in fomenting the American revolt.[4]

---

1   E Pound, *America, Roosevelt & the Causes of the Present War,* op. cit., 6.

2   E Pound, *Social Credit: An Impact,* op. cit., 8.

3   E Pound, *A Visiting Card,* op. cit., 16.

4   Ibid., 10.

Guernsey

One of the most successful and enduring examples of usury-free state credit has been that of Guernsey, British Channel Islands, whose banking experiment was initiated in 1820. Guernsey's banking system was prompted by dire need, the island being in serious financial trouble from the beginning of the 19th Century. Guernsey's town was undeveloped, the roads were cart-tracks, and there was no prospect for employment. The most serious problem however was the encroaching sea that was washing away large tracts of land because of the disrepair of the dykes. Neither tax increases nor further loans were practicable.

However it was the need to upgrade the Public Market that prompted a committee to report back with a solution in 1816 to issue £6000 worth of States Notes.[5] The committee also recommended that the States Notes be used not only for the new market, but also for Torteval Church, road construction and other State expenses. The notes' issue was started in 1820, and was followed by other issues, until by 1837 £55,000 of the Notes were in circulation, debt-free and having created prosperity and development, which in turn stimulated visitors to the island.[6]

Of course there were complaints to the Privy Council that such debt-free issues were being made, but the States Financial Committee gave such good account of the island that the objections were unsuccessful. However two banks on the island flooded Guernsey with their own notes to undermine the State Notes, and for reasons unknown it was the Island that agreed to limit the issue of its Notes.[7] It was such a tactic used by the North to undermine the Graybacks of the South during the American Civil War that caused inflationary problems, but these manoeuvres do not discredit the efficacy of state credit. With the outbreak of war in 1914 Guernsey restarted the Notes issue according to requirements. While State Notes continue

---

5   Olive and Jan Grubiak, *The Guernsey Experiment* (ca. 1960), 7.

6   Ibid. 8-9.

7   Ibid., 10.

to circulate alongside British Pounds Sterling there has never been inflation, and the prosperity of the island continues as it has since 1820[8], operating on minimal taxation.[9]

The Wära

Like Guernsey a century previously, a 'free money' movement was started in Germany in 1919, in the aftermath of the world war, based on the ideas of the unorthodox economic theorist Silvio Gesell, who advocated a type of voucher currency to keep up consumption. In an attempt to eliminate its war debts German currency had been inflated and had brought ruin to ordinary folk. This hyperinflation, with the often-cited image of a barrow load of currency being wheeled to pay for a loaf of bread, is frequently used to claim that state currency causes inflation. This is nonsense. It was the debt system that caused Germany's hyperinflation, ruining the working and middle classes, while international bankers continued to reap the rewards of debt. A period of deflation followed, stagnating the economy.

The American economist Professor Irving Fisher of Yale University, stated that in 1926 Hans Timms, a friend of Gesell's established the Wära Barter Company, which issued its own 'scrip', the Wära. He stated that Wära was a word compounded of two others, 'Ware' and 'Währung', meaning respectively 'Goods' and 'Currency'. It is an apt name for a token that was intended to function as all currency and credit should: to exchange goods.

By October 1929, the year of the Wall Street Crash, the Company had issued Wära in five denominations, which could be purchased with an equivalent amount of Reichsmarks.[10] In 1930, with the

---

8   According to World Travel Guide, Guernsey Exchange Rate, 'Guernsey has its own currency... Channel Islands notes and coins are not accepted in the UK, although they can be converted in parity at UK banks.' www.worldtravelguide.net/country/108/money/Europe/Guernsey.html

9   Ibid. 11.

10   Irving Fisher, *Stamp Scrip* (New York: Adelphi Publishers, 1933), Chapter IV: the First

Great Depression hitting Germany with full force, causing massive unemployment, Hebecker, the owner of a disused coal mine in the town of Schwanenkirchen, with a population of 500, borrowed 40,000 Reichsmarks from the Wära Barter Company, and issued the equivalent amount of vouchers for his coal. The miners were persuaded to accept the Wära as wages, which were in turn accepted by the village trades people, because they were redeemable as coal from Hebecker or, if necessary, as Reichsmarks. The Wära vouchers levied a fee of 1% every month on the holder, paid to the coal mine and used to fund the publicising of the system; therefore it was in the interests of the voucher holders to keep spending them into circulation prior to arrival of the month's tax.

Schwanenkirchen prospered while the rest of Germany fell into destitution. Reporters from all over Germany descended on the village to write about the 'miracle'. Even although the number in circulation was never more than 20,000 Wära, because they were kept in circulation, 2.5 million people used them as a means of exchange.

Experiments Abroad: Silvio Gesell, www.userpage.fu-berlin.de/~roehrigw/fisher/stamp4.html

The Wära currency spread throughout Germany, and was accepted and backed with different commodities by 2000 corporations. In November 1931 the Government passed an emergency law prohibiting the Wära, and the condition of unemployment and destitution was resumed.[11]

Woergl

Woergl, an Austrian town of 4300, where factories were closing down, followed the example of Schwanenkirchen, and the Mayor, Unterguggenberger, formed a Local Relief Committee, not to dispense charity but to create work. Professor Fisher states of this:

> Herr Unterguggenberger had watched the Schwanenkirchen Wara experiment with intense interest. The solution of the Woergl situation pointed to Stamp Scrip. The town would issue it, with the consent of the workmen and of a sufficient number of the merchants and also of the local savings bank. The bank was to hold the guarantee fund (in the form as previously described of a bookkeeping transaction). There was to be no final redemption; and the stamps, at 1 per cent per month, were to be sold by the town, and the proceeds used ... for the enlargement of the town's welfare work. But though there was to be no final and complete redemption, every holder of the scrip was to have the privilege of redeeming it at the town treasury or at the local banks at any time; but for such redemption a service charge of two per cent had to be paid. As the stamp was only 1 per cent, the disadvantages of redemption at 2 per cent were, at any given moment, greater than the probable disadvantages of going on at 1 per cent. Redemption, therefore, was not likely to hurt the circulation of the scrip. Moreover the banks and the town were to re-issue any that was redeemed. And so it worked out in practice.

---

11   Ibid.

All city employees, including the mayor, were to receive 50 per cent of their salaries in scrip, and the new emergency workmen, were to be paid 100 per cent in that form. According to plan, on August 1, 1932, 32,000 Schillings' worth of the scrip (equivalent to about $4500) was issued, in denominations of 1, 5 and 10 Schillings. This amount was later found to be in excess of the actual need, and instead of following an 'inflationary' policy, only about 1/3 of the issue or less was kept in circulation through re-issues, the rest remained with the city. This showed great wisdom on the part of the municipal administration, as it kept the purchasing power of scrip at par with regular Schillings. The scrip was called 'Woergl Certified Compensation Bills'. The monthly stamps (affixed to the face of the scrip) were named 'Relief Contribution Stamps', and each unit of scrip was super-scribed, 'They Alleviate Want, Give Work and Bread'. What were the results?[12]

Fisher, who had sent at observer to Woergl, reported that in the first half of 1932, new public works had been initiated, streets were rebuilt, the sewer system extended, trees planted and forests improved, and rather than a rise, there was a drop in unemployed. Further:

---

12   Ibid., 'Woergl'.

On January 1, 1933 Woergl (which is an Alpine town) had under construction a new ski jump and a water basin for the Fire Department. The mayor says that the scrip has fulfilled all promises, and thinks it should be adopted nationally. At all events, a neighboring city of 20,000 inhabitants, was, at last reports, considering the introduction of scrip within its borders, under the advice of the mayor of Woergl and of a University Professor of economics, and the Woergl experiment has begun to attract somewhat general attention in Austria. As conclusion to this report Mayor Unterguggenberger stated: 'The Stamp Scrip of Woergl will have historic significance, because it has kept its promise to provide "work and bread". It has, in fact fully satisfied all our expectations".[13]

Austrian courts prohibited the Stamp Scrip on 1 September 1933.[14] The Woergl experiment was emulated in US towns during the Great Depression, led by the town of Hawarden, Iowa. Fisher wrote:

This is a town of 3000 inhabitants. Its finances were in good shape, but there were plenty of workless men and the usual number of boarders. So, in October 1932, upon petition, the town decided to issue $300 in Stamp Scrip of $1.00 denomination. The sum was to be used principally for a town road to be built by otherwise workless men.[15]

Fisher reported on the use of 'Scrip' in other towns and cities across the USA during the Great Depression, and efforts to get US Congress to issue Scrip nationally.[16]

---

13   Ibid.

14   Michael Unterguggenberger, Burgomaster of Wörgl (Austria), 'The End Result of the Woergl Experiment', Annals of Collective Economy, Geneva, Switzerland, 1934 www.reinventingmoney.com/worglUnter.php

15   Irving Fisher, Stamp Scrip, op. cit., Chapter V: 'The Sudden Spread of 'Scrip' in the United States, www.userpage.fu-berlin.de/~roehrigw/fisher/stamp5.html

16   Ibid.

Scrip issue showed that currency could be issued that was not 'inflationary', and that served as a permanently circulating stimulus to the economy. As will be seen, the Governor of Quebec in the 18th Century undertook a similar scheme with the ingenious expedient of circulating cut up playing cards when he lacked even a printing press to print a scrip. Guernsey Island issued its own currency when faced with bankruptcy in the early 19th century, and continues to circulate its own currency. The Social Credit Government of Alberta, Canada, put into circulation 'Prosperity Certificates' when the Central Government stymied its efforts at every turn to fulfil its election platform of creating a Social Credit economy.

Communities, and indeed whole states and nations overcame economic collapse by rejecting the orthodox economic path of debt, and issuing state or local currencies, scrip, certificates, vouchers, and credit as the requirements of the economy necessitated. They did so without causing the orthodox bugbear of 'inflation', and achieved recovery while others around them languished in 'poverty', killed livestock and dumped food while people went hungry for lack of purchasing power. While the 'modern economy' now uses computers rather than ledger books, the principles remain the same; the problems are the same, and the solutions are the same. What has changed is that there now exists fewer visionary leaders than ever, and a mass of public ignorance on the subject of banking in this supposedly more 'educated' age.

Commonwealth Bank Of Australia

A state bank was inaugurated primarily thanks to the tireless efforts of iconic Labor politician King O'Malley. O'Malley was a Christian when it was possible to be both a Christian and a 'socialist' and 'socialism' was not synonymous with Marxist atheism. In many ways his struggle to break the hold of usury over Australia was similar to that of New Zealand iconic Labour politician John A Lee, who is discussed below. Like Lee, O'Malley often found himself opposed by the 'socialists' in his own party. O'Malley began campaigning for an Australian state bank in 1901 as a Member of Parliament in Tasmania.

From then until 1910 O'Malley was the only Member of Parliament to speak in detail on this. Finally in 1908 the Brisbane Labor Party conference adopted O'Malley's scheme that became the basis of the Commonwealth Bank.[17]

In 1908 O'Malley presented his scheme in full to Parliament, for the purposes of creating a 'National Bank of Deposit, Issue, Exchange and Reserve'.[18] A biographer states in regard to the opposition that O'Malley encountered for a state bank within the highest echelon's of the Labor Party:

> In 1908 O'Malley presented to parliament a detailed plan for the creation of a national bank of deposit, issue, exchange and reserve, and in the same year at the third Federal conference of the A.L.P. succeeded in transferring creation of a 'Commonwealth Bank' to the fighting platform. Despite this, O'Malley knew that many party members were lukewarm and he devoted the next two years to educating them. Partly because of his bad relations with Prime Minister Fisher and W. M. Hughes, O'Malley was not elected by caucus to the ministry in 1908. Fisher

---

17   King O'Malley, *The Commonwealth Bank: The Facts and its Creation*, introductory remarks.

18   Ibid., 'Financial Relations of the Commonwealth and the States', Presented to Parliament by command, April 15, 1908, 1 (1).

and Hughes were not convinced of the need for a national bank before the government was defeated in June 1909. But party support was growing for a competing bank that would smash the 'Money Power'.[19]

O'Malley, like New Zealand's John A Lee, had a sound knowledge of banking practices which he explained when introducing the scheme:

The present banking system was founded on the idea that the many were created for the few to prey on. Debts are contracted for land, labor, products, and other commodities. When interest rises Government Bonds depreciate; holders sell to secure ready money to benefit by rise in interest. High rates of interest rapidly increase the indebtedness of the people. Their wealth is soon transferred to the few privileged capitalists who are enabled to control the rate of interest, and consequently the market value of Government Bonds and property. As long as money may be obtained on good security at a reasonable rate of interest per annum Government Bonds will command at least their par value.

The present banking system is operated to enrich bankers and a few capitalists, instead of operating for the benefit of the producers. The interest collected on the endorsed promissory notes of the producers maintains the banks and pays all their extravagant expenditure in superb buildings and Directorial salaries and dividends to shareholders. The banks, under Parliamentary sanction, make the people furnish the capital, and then pay interest on this capital. Although the industry of the producers supports the whole, they have no voice in the management. All the gains of the banks by the rise of interest is a special tax on the industry of the producers for the benefit of financiers.

---

19   Arthur Hoyle, 'O'Malley, King (1858–1953)', *Australian Dictionary of Biography*, National Centre of Biography, Australian National University, www.adb.anu.edu.au/biography/omalley-king-7907/text13753

If the banks were established on a Christian basis they could loan credit to assist the productive industry of the Commonwealth at low rates of interest, instead of making loans which are in turn re-loaned at high rates of interest. No financial crises in the monetary affairs of the country could then be possible.

Our banking system rests on a false basis — promising to redeem in gold, which is impossible. Therefore, the money mongers can create a financial crisis whenever it suits their business by demanding and forcing the banks to suspend specie payments; and in order to prevent this, the banks earmark credit for them at the expense of the producers.

Frenzied financiers work in each other's interests, and secure the last farthing from the producers of the wealth of the Commonwealth under the pretence that the money or the bullion is the real wealth, and, they keep the producers permanently toiling for gold without possessing it, while they live in luxury on what the workers produce.

A small amount of money is always capable of paying a large amount of promissory notes, bonds, debts, or mortgages; also buying every description of property. The money which pays for one farm may also pay for a second, a third, and a fourth on the same day.

Banks gain as much by the deposits left with them as they would by the circulation of interest equal amount of bank notes. As a rule, they pay no interest on current deposits, and they lend their deposits to traders and producers and others and charge interest on them.[20]

O'Malley's description of the banking system in 1908 continues to apply to today's banking methods. Note here that O'Malley appeals to 'Christianity', not Marxism, which has never

20   King O'Malley, op. cit., 'Reasons for a Commonwealth Bank'.

had much to say on banking, and obscures the real causes of economic crises, exploitation and dispossession by focusing on private property rather than on banking and usury. O'Malley then described how the banking system creates booms and busts through the manipulation of credit:

The banks may make money very plentiful or very scarce. The banks may make good endorsed security notes and sell at a big discount. When banks are extending their credits they encourage producers and traders to open accounts with them, being glad to expand overdrafts to any reasonable amount. Suddenly the speculators produce an apparent scarcity of money by earmarking all the available credit; consequently the banks must cease extending overdrafts to the small producers and traders. The banks assure customers that money is tight, while in reality there has been no diminution in the amount of money, nor have the amounts of discounts been increased.

The financiers keep in their own hands the power to make the money market tighter that they may re-loan to the producers and traders at higher rates of interest. If for only one day the bank's loan only one-half of the usual amounts it is felt in the money Market. All unsupplied producers and traders must secure money elsewhere, no matter how high the rate of interest.

They are driven to the money mongers to be skinned, while the money mongers secure from the banks at low interest. The paper they had discounted when money was plentiful is maturing and must be redeemed. The money mongers charge them 12 to 20 per cent., and discount their paper at the banks for current rates.

The small producers and traders have no option but to pay whatever interest the money mongers demand. The inevitable result — bankruptcy.

Directors in banks and financial institutions (use) the power to paralyze their weaker opponents, through their ability to borrow.

The value of all kinds of State securities shrink; Capitalists call in their loans at low rates of interest and invest in these securities at greatly reduced prices.

If money were plentiful and the rate of interest uniform there would be no inducement to sacrifice one class of investment in order to secure another.

The apparent scarcity of money soon speaks throughout the Commonwealth and the money mongers take advantage of the borrowers.[21]

O'Malley stated that with opposition within the Labor Party to his proposals against usury, he 'continued to secretly organize the Commonwealth Bank fight'. Like New Zealand's Lee, against the wishes of the Labor Cabinet, having become Minister of Home Affairs in 1910, he appealed to the Caucus in 1911, and was overwhelmingly supported. His scheme became part of the Government's programme. [22]

The Commonwealth Bank, however, was constituted to act as a regular commercial bank, albeit state-owned (like New Zealand's current Kiwi Bank), and not as the generator of state credit. It was as the British economist Alexander Raven Thomson, cited previously, described such 'socialist' measures: limited at best if banks are not given the prerogative to create credit. Like the Reserve Banks of today, the Commonwealth Bank was merely intended by Fisher to serve as the state agency for borrowing from private banking. However, the first Governor of the bank, Sir Denison Miller, proceeded to operate the bank without recourse to private capital, but on the security of the nation's credit, based on actual savings deposits. The Commonwealth Bank was therefore able to fund Australia's infrastructure for decades, on

---

21   Ibid., 'Millions to Loan'.

22   Ibid, 'Caucus Action'.

the people's credit, without usury. An Australian commentator remarks on the achievements of the Commonwealth Bank:

> ... At a time when private banks were demanding 6% interest for loans, the Commonwealth Bank financed Australia's first world war effort from 1914 to 1919 with a loan of $700,000,000 at an interest rate of a fraction of 1%, thus saving Australians some $12 million in bank charges. In 1916 it made funds available in London to purchase 15 cargo steamers to support Australia's growing export trade. Until 1924 the benefits conferred upon the people of Australia by their Bank flowed steadily on. It financed jam and fruit pools to the extent of $3 million, it found $8 million for Australian homes, while to local government bodies, for construction of roads, tramways, harbours, gasworks, electric power plants, etc., it lent $18.72 million. It paid $6.194 million to the Commonwealth Government between December, 1920 and June, 1923 - the profits of its Note Issue Department - while by 1924 it had made on its other business a profit of $9 million, available for redemption of debt. The bank's independently-minded Governor, Sir Denison Miller, used the bank's credit power after the First World War to save Australians from the depression conditions being imposed in other countries.[23]

In 1924 the governing of the Bank was placed in the hands of a directorate comprised mainly of private interests, and the work that the Bank had undertaken previously was stymied.[24] Hence, while across the Tasman the Reserve Bank of New Zealand issued state credit for the iconic state housing scheme in 1935, Australians were denied the same benefits that their Commonwealth Bank could have implemented had the intentions of O'Malley been enacted. Indeed, by the Depression era, the Commonwealth Bank even refused to extend credit

---

23   David Kidd, 'How Money is created in Australia', www.archive.org/
web/20010714001752/http:/dkd.net/davekidd/politics/money.html

24   Ibid.

to the Scullin Labor Government unless pensions were cut, which Scullin refused. During World War II the State resumed its authority over the Bank and in the aftermath of the war it oversaw economic expansion. The bank was privatised during the 1990s.[25]

New Zealand

The election of the First New Zealand Labour Government centred on its platform of nationalizing the Reserve Bank and issuing state credit. The 1934 Commonwealth tour by Maj. C H Douglas had a major impact, and in New Zealand organisations such as the Auckland Farmers' Union and the New Zealand Legion adopted Social Credit. In particular the flamboyant, one-armed war veteran John A Lee kept up a continuous agitation for the Labour Party to fulfil its election promises despite the resistance of Prime Minister Joseph Savage and his Finance Minister Walter Nash. Lee had written several pamphlets on banking reform which should serve today as seminal references for banking reformers, but are forgotten.

John A Lee

The first of Lee's pamphlets, *Money Power for the People*, outlined his ideas on what he hoped the Labour Government would adopt as legislative policy, based upon what the party had presented to voters at the 1935 General Election as official party policy.[26] This was the demand for the 'immediate control by the State of the entire banking system', including the 'state issue of credit for production and distribution of commodities'.[27] The party's manifesto for the election stated:

---

25 Ellen Brown, 'What a Government can do with its own Bank', http://www.webofdebt. com/articles/commonwealth_bank_aus.php

26 J A Lee, *Money Power for the People* (Auckland: Lee, 1937).

27 J A Lee, *A Letter which Every New Zealander Should Read* (Auckland: A B Parker, 1939), 7.

'Soup Kitchen' - Wellington, New Zealand 1934.

A planned economy will be of little use if the Government has not the power to carry its plans into effect. Such power will require the control of credit which, if it remains in private hands, can be used to thwart the will of the Government .[28]

The Great Depression was a period in which, unlike today with our supposedly more educated populations, people were all talking about questions of finance and banking reform. Lee recalled that the largest political meetings in New Zealand history had been held throughout New Zealand, and the question to the fore was that of money. He vividly related, 'Wherever people were gathered', whether on street corner, in the factory, stock yard or on a tram, 'there was discussion about banking and money'.[29]

In *Money Power for the People*, which might be seen as a reminder to the party Caucus of its election pledges, Lee stated that the first meeting of the Labour Cabinet in Office in 1936

28   J A Lee, ibid., 8.

29   J A Lee, *Money Power for the People*, op. cit. 1.

reaffirmed its commitment to 'winning complete financial power as the first move toward a new social order'. Parliament met in March and the following month the Government introduced the Reserve Bank of New Zealand Amendment Bill.[30] The Bill was supposed to reform the Reserve Bank that had been established in 1933, on the prompting of the Bank of England, as a corporation that included private stockholders, with the directors being a mix of those nominated by the state and those elected by the stockholders. The bank was independent from the State, despite theoretically being a State Bank, at least in the popular imagination, like the Federal Reserve Bank in the USA or the Bank of England. This 1936 Bank amendment bought the private stockholders out 'at a handsome profit', the bank came under State control, and the Board of Directors became 'the direct servant of the Government of the day', who were obliged to fulfill the policies of Government and were subject to removal. The Bank's function set out in Section 1 of the Act was to 'regulate and control credit and currency in New Zealand' for the 'economic and social welfare of New Zealand'.[31]

The second part of *Money Power for the People* deals with what the Labour Government had achieved over the past year. Lee stated that the Government's powers had been used cautiously, but that state credit was being provided to the dairy industry account, which worked with the state's control of the marketing of produce (through marketing boards), and hence there was a guaranteed price for farmers.[32] The Reserve Bank issued the dairy industry state credit, at minor profit, where hitherto the private banks had gained through interest, with the additional factor that the profits that were made by the State on these advances were placed back into a Consolidated Fund. The aim was to eventually reduce the amount of interest to a charge for costs only.[33]

---

30   Ibid., 5.

31   Ibid., 6.

32   Ibid., 8.

33   Ibid.

Nonetheless, despite these great reforms, the Government was still borrowing from overseas moneylenders; a matter that was never resolved. This is precisely what Alexander Raven Thomson had warned of when stating that 'socialist' measures to nationalise banking were not enough if those state-run banks still borrowed from private finance. Hence, the Left when nationalising banks could present themselves as the champions of 'the people' against 'capitalism', while in reality nothing changed.

The power to create credit was – and remains – often with the international bankers regardless of whether the bank is state-run or private. That is the great con of capitalism and socialism working in tandem, and it is why states that have been run for many years by 'socialists', such as Greece, are indebted to the point of bankruptcy and must go about selling their assets to diminish those debts.

Lee warned that unless the State assumed sole responsibility for creating and issuing credit, 'the debt will be compounded forever' and that 'at some future date the Capitalist bailiff will liquidate New Zealand's social experiment'. That is precisely what happened when a 'free market revolution' proceeded decades later under a Labour Government, in a typical example of socialists playing lackey to international finance. New Zealand is still in the process of divesting itself of what few state assets remain to pay off debt, and the international debt crisis now grips most of the world, including the theoretically 'wealthiest', the USA.

State Housing

However, it was a great achievement in the funding of the iconic state housing project with Reserve Bank state credit, this one measure being sufficient to resolve 75% of unemployment in the midst of the Great Depression. Lee commented in his 1937 assessment that so far the State Housing project was the only program on which the State had availed itself the prerogative to issue its own credit. An initial £5,000,000[34] of state credit through the Reserve Bank was issued for housing via the Housing Account of the State Advances Corporation.[35] Lee cites Finance Minister Nash as stating to Parliament that the credit would be state issued in entirety as 'new money' on which the interest earned in its entirety would return to the State as profit, while the houses would remain in State ownership. In a Government document over a decade later the project was explained as follows:

Reserve Bank Credit: To finance its comprehensive proposals, the Government adopted the somewhat unusual course of using Reserve Bank credit, thus recognising that the most important factor in housing costs is the price of money – interest is the heaviest portion in the composition of ordinary rent. The newly created Department was able therefore to obtain the use of funds at the lowest possible rate of interest, the rate being 1% for the first £10 million advanced, and one and a half percent on further advances. The sums advanced by the Reserve Bank were not subscribed or underwritten by other financial institutions. This action shaped the Government's intention to demonstrate that it is possible for the State to use the country's credit in creating new assets for the country.[36]

This was achieved without causing inflation, or any of the other objections leveled against so-called 'funny money'. This, and many of the other examples discussed here, has been put down the Memory Hole. The use of state credit is a forgotten part of New Zealand history, yet the state housing scheme is widely lauded. What is forgotten is the mechanism by which the state houses were funded. It is about as submerged from

---

34   E Olssen, *John A Lee* (Dunedin, New Zealand: Otago University Press, 1977), 93.

35   J A Lee, *Money Power for the People*, op. cit., 10.

36   C Firth and G Wilson, *State Housing in New Zealand* (Wellington: Government Printing Office, 1949).

memory as the banking reforms of National Socialist Germany, Imperial Japan or Fascist Italy. Professor Paul Moon, one of New Zealand's better class of academics nonetheless does not so much as mention Reserve Bank credit in his discussion of state housing in his recent book on epochal events of New Zealand history.[37]

Today, with Christchurch, South Island, New Zealand, needing reconstruction after two large earthquakes, the Government dithers, lacking money, unable to organise or finance a massive construction project to undertake what is urgently needed. There is huge unemployment as there was during the Great Depression, there are tradesmen who need jobs, there are houses that need building or fixing, and yet nothing is done because the Government does not believe in interfering with 'market forces' or issuing state credit.

Canada

In 1935 the Social Credit Party took Office in Alberta, Canada, under the Premiership of William Aberhart. Both C H Douglas and John Hargrave advised the Government. Despite the overwhelming demand of Albertans, Canada's central Government stymied the Social Credit legislation that had been passed by the Provincial Parliament, at every occasion.[38] In 1937 the Social Credit Government passed 'An Act to Provide the Realization of Social Credit in Alberta', which received assent in 1938. Under the Act a Social Credit Board was established.[39] However, in March of that year the Supreme Court of Canada determined that it was not within the jurisdiction of a Province

---

37　Paul Moon, *Turning Points*: Events That Changed the Course of New Zealand History (New Holland Press, 2013) 149-152.

38　'Summary of 1937 Social Credit Legislation', http://www.aberhartfoundation.ca/ PDF%20Documents/Social%20Credit%20Statues/Government%201937%20SC%20 Act%20Summary.pdf

39　'An Act to Provide the Realization of Social Credit in Alberta', http://www. aberhartfoundation.ca/PDF%20Documents/Social%20Credit%20Statues/An%20 Act%20To%20Provide%20the%20Realization%20of%20the%20Social%20Credit%20 of%20Alberta.pdf

to legislate on currency.[40] What the Alberta Government could do was issue 'Prosperity Certificate's circumventing the Central Government's obstructionism and allowing for the increased flow of credit among the people. Such 'Scrip' bills had been and were being similarly issued by local authorities in Canadian and in US townships, with examples going back to the era of the American Colonies.[41]

However, from 1935 Canada did maintain a state credit system lasting into the 1970s. The state-owned Bank of Canada issued up to half of all new money at low interest, which in turn forced the commercial banks to keep interest rates low. This resulted in decades of prosperity. From 1935-1939 the Bank of Canada was issuing **most** of the nation's credit, and 62% of the credit during the last years of the War. Until the mid 1970s the Canadian Government continued to create enough new state money to monetarize 20% to 30% of the state deficit.

That ratio is now only 7.5%. While the money supply increases by $22 billion annually, the Bank of Canada now issues less than

---

40 'Disallowance of Three Social Credit of Alberta Bills', 4 March 1938, http://www. aberhartfoundation.ca/PDF%20Documents/Premier%20PDF%27s/Legislation-Court%20Rulings/Mar4th,1938%20Sup_Ct%20Disallow3bills.pdf

41 'Scrip Notes', http://www.aberhartfoundation.ca/Pages/LargeScripPage.htm

2% of that money. It has been estimated that if the Canadian Government had continued to operate such a financial system as she had for around three decades, that nation would today be operating with a surplus of $13 billion.[42]

Germany

Propaganda rather than scholarship has dominated studies on National Socialist Germany. Hence, the manner by which certain socioeconomic achievements were attained is buried amidst histories that focus on war, the Holocaust, and racial theories. Where the economic recovery of Germany during the Depression era is noted at all it is simplistically accounted for by spending on rearmament, which by itself explains nothing.

If the British Commonwealth states had their C H Douglas, the pre-eminent advocate of Germany's liberation from usury was Gottfried Feder. The National Socialist party just happened to be the movement that was the vehicle for advocating Feder's views. Although Feder had taken his state credit scheme to the extreme Left, it was of no interest to the Marxist 'revolutionaries'. His theories might have been enacted by the Weimer regime, which showed interest, but the Republic did not have the determination. Feder was a lecturer for the army, and it is in that capacity that he was heard by Adolf Hitler.[43]

Gottfried Feder

As early as 1917 – that is, the same year that Douglas had first formulated Social Credit – Feder started advocating banking

---

42   Harold Chorney, Associate Professor of Political Economy and Public Policy, Concordia University, Montreal; John Hotson, Professor of Economics, University of Waterloo; Mario Seccareccia, Assoc. Professor of Economics, University of Ottawa; *The Deficit Made Me Do It!*, 'Introduction', CCPA Popular Economics Series, Editor: Ed Finn, Canadian Centre For Policy Alternatives, 2010. http://lists.topica.com/lists/VOW/read/message.html?mid=813781210&sort=d&start=6327

43   J Toland, *Adolf Hitler* (New York: Doubleday, 1970), 83.

reform,[44] and formed the Fighting League Against Interest Slavery. Feder's *Manifesto for the Breaking of the Bondage of Interest* was published the following year. In this he stated that the source of the power of the international banking system 'is the effortless and infinite multiplication of wealth which is created by interest'. He recommended that the 'drones' 'living off productive people's and their labour' be eliminated by 'breaking the bondage of interest':

> Money is not and must not be anything but an exchange for labour; that to be sure any highly developed country does need money as a medium of exchange, but that this exhausts the function of money, and can in no case give to money, through interest, a supernatural power to reproduce itself at the costs of productive labour.[45]

Feder had been a founder-member of the German Workers' Party prior to Hitler's recruitment. The earliest policy document of the German Workers' Party[46] shows opposition to usury to have been a premise of the group from the start. The party rejected socialization of production in favour of 'profit-sharing' and co-operatives. To the question 'who is the DAP fighting against?' the reply was:

> The DAP is fighting with all its strength against usury and the forcing up of prices. Against all those who create no values, who make high profits without any mental or physical work.[47]

---

44 B M Lane and L J Rupp, *Nazi Ideology Before 1933* (Manchester University Press, 1978), 148.

45 Gottfried Feder, *Manifesto for Breaking the Bondage of Interest*, reprinted in B M Lane and L J Rupp, ibid., p. 27-30. The Feder manifesto has recently been reprinted and is available at: Historical Review Press, http://www.historicalreviewpress.com/manifesto-for-the-breaking-of-the-financial-slavery-to-usury-by-gottfried-feder-590-p.asp

46 Deutsche Arbeiterpartei (DAP).

47 'Guideline of the German Workers' Party', January 5, 1919. B M Lane and L J Rupp, op. cit., 10.

The People's Car - Adolf Hitler visits the "Volkswagen" factory 1938.

The German Workers' Party, in common with Rightists and conservative revolutionaries such as Oswald Spengler, recognised from the start the nexus between international finance and the Left, including the communists. Another early DAP statement, *'To All Working People!'*, was written by the eminent playwright Deitrich Eckart. At the time of the creation of the Munich Soviet, Eckart distributed his essay as a leaflet on the streets in an effort to win the masses away from the short-lived Soviet Republic. The leaflet was republished in 1924, and by Feder in 1933, when he identified himself as co-author.[48] Eckart and Feder point out that despite the revolutionary tumult created by the Marxists, this was the primary issue and it was ignored by the Marxists in the clamour for the abolition of private property. But 'loan capital', and 'nothing but this!', is the cause of a nation's and an individual's burden. They continued:

Loan capital brings in money without work, brings it in through interest. I repeat: without lifting a finger the capitalist increases his wealth by lending his money. It grows by itself.

---

48   B M Lane and L J Rupp, ibid., 30.

No matter how lazy one is, if one has money enough and lends it out at interest, one can live high and one's children don't need to work either, or one's grandchildren, or one's great-great grandchildren, and so on to eternity! How unjust this is, how shameless – doesn't everyone feel it?

To infinity it grows, this loan capital...

But who provides them [the House of Rothschild] and their like with such an enormous amount of money? Interest has to come from somewhere after all, somewhere these billions and more billions have to be produced by hard labour! Who does this? You do it, nobody but you! That's right, it is your money, hard earned through care and sorrow, which is as if magnetically drawn into the coffers of these insatiable people...[49]

The twenty-five point 'Program of the NSDAP', formulated the following year again reflected the doctrines of Feder. Among these points are:

10. It must be the duty of every citizen to work either mentally or physically. The activities of the individual may not conflict with the interests of the general public but must be carried on within the framework of the whole and for the good of all.

WE THEREFORE DEMAND

11. Abolition of income unearned by labour or effort;

BREAKING THE BONDAGE OF INTEREST.[50]

It was after hearing a lecture given by Feder to the political

49   D Eckart and G Feder, 'To all Working People', Munich, April 5, 1919; B M Lane and L J Rupp, ibid., 30-31.

50   'The Program of the NSDAP', 24 February 1920. B M Lane and L J Rupp, ibid., 42.

agents of the army that Hitler stated: 'Right after listening to Feder's first lecture, the thought ran through my head that I had now found the way to one of the most essential premises for the foundation of a new party'.[51]

It is a pity that groups and individuals on the Right do not recall or know this, and cannot get beyond 'white power' or 'anti-Semitism'. By inane obsessions the Right is missing the historical boat at the very juncture that the 'loan capital' system should be fought most vigorously.

State Credit and Barter

How then did Germany 'break the bondage of interest'? Professor A J P Taylor, the eminent British historian, and hardly a Nazi sympathizer, writes:

> Fascism, it was claimed, represented the last aggressive stage of capitalism in decline, and its momentum could be sustained only by war. There was an element of truth in this, but not much. The full employment which Nazi Germany was the first European country to possess, depended in large part on the production of armaments; but it could have been provided equally well (and was to some extent) by other forms of public works from roads to great buildings. The Nazi secret was not armament production; it was freedom from the then orthodox principles of economics… the argument for war did not work even if the Nazi system had relied on armaments production alone. Nazi Germany was not choking in a flood of arms. On the contrary, the German Generals insisted unanimously in 1939 that they were not equipped for war and that many years must pass before 'rearmament in depth' had been completed.[52]

---

51   J Toland, op. cit., 83-84.

52   A J P Taylor, *The Origins of the Second World War* (New York: Fawcett Premier, 1961), 103-104.

Yet even Taylor, whose book is interesting in its repudiation of the 'sole war guilt' doctrine, fails to understand exactly how Germany achieved recovery. Despite what Taylor states about Hitler lacking a consistent policy, the views on loan capital and the stock exchange were features of his speeches before and after assuming Government. Hitler's speech of 30 January 1939 to the Reichstag is perhaps the most informative he made on the principles upon which Germany was being reconstructed. Answering predictions of ruin by orthodox economists throughout the world, Hitler explained that Germany had not withdrawn from world trade but had bypassed the international financial system by means of barter, stating:

If certain countries combat the German system this is done in the first instance because through the German method of trading their tricks of international currency and Bourse speculations have been abolished in favour of honest business transactions... We are buyers of good foodstuff and raw materials and suppliers of equally good commodities![53]

Taylor comments on German trade barter:

Germany was not short of markets. On the contrary, Schacht[54] used bilateral agreements to give Germany practically a monopoly of trade with south-eastern Europe; and similar plans were being prepared for the economic conquest of South America when the outbreak of war interrupted them.[55]

It should be reiterated here that according to no less than Franklin D Roosevelt, as recorded by his son Elliott, the American President reminded Winston Churchill that the war against Germany had been fought over the issue of Germany's

---

53 A Hitler, Reichstag speech, January 30, 1939. R de Roussy de Sales (ed.) Adolf Hitler: *My New Order*, (London: Angus and Robertson, 1942), 457.

54 Hjalmar Schacht, President of the Reichsbank.

55 A J P Taylor, op. cit. 105.

capturing the markets of world trade. As stated, Germany was achieving this prior to the war by bypassing the international financial system and bartering surplus products between states. Roosevelt said to Churchill:

> 'Of course, after the war, one of the preconditions of any lasting peace will have to be the greatest possible freedom of trade. No artificial barriers....' Roosevelt stated that imperial trade agreements would have to go, and remarked that the Third Reich's incursion into European trade had been a major cause of the war.[56] Churchill, the impotent 'war horse' spoke in despair, 'Mr. President, I believe you are trying to do away with the British Empire. Every idea you entertain about the structure of the post-war world demonstrates it'.[57]

Thus, according to the definitive statement of President Roosevelt, the real reason for the war against Germany was to destroy Germany's alternative trade and financial policies that were undermining control by international finance. Furthermore, independent trading blocs, such as the old European empires, were not going to be tolerated in the post-war era. Additionally, the well-informed and connected Hasting W S Russell, Marquis of Tavistock, (later the 12th Duke of Bedford), who was a pacifist and a monetary reformer, wrote at the start of the war that it is:

> A war of financiers and fools, though most people, on the allied side at any rate, do not yet see very clearly how financiers come into it. ...Financiers also desired war as a means of overthrowing their rivals and consolidating still further the immense power... Hitler not only engaged in barter trade which meant no discount profits for bankers arranging bills of Exchange, but he even went so far as to declare that a country's real wealth consisted in its ability to produce goods; nor, when men and material were

---

56   Elliott Roosevelt, *As He Saw It*, op. cit., 35.

57   Ibid. 31.

available, would he ever allow lack of money to be an obstacle in the way of any project which he considered to be in his country's interests. This was rank heresy in the eyes of the financiers of Britain and America, a heresy which, if allowed to spread, would blow the gaff on the whole financial racket.[58]

Hitler explained precisely the foundations of the new economic and financial system:

If ever need makes humans see clearly it has made the German people do so. Under the compulsion of this need we have learned in the first place to take full account of the most essential capital of a nation, namely, its capacity to work. All thoughts of a gold reserves and foreign exchange fade before the industry and efficiency of well-planned national productive resources. We can smile today at an age when economists were seriously of the opinion that the value of currency was determined by the reserves of gold and foreign exchange lying in the vaults of the national banks and, above all, was guaranteed by them. Instead of that we have learned to realize that the value of a currency lies in a nation's power of production, that an increasing volume of production sustains a currency, and could possibly raise its value, whereas a decreasing production must, sooner or later, lead to a compulsory devaluation...[59]

One of the few places where National Socialist Germany's economic policies were plainly explained was in New Zealand, and it might be observed that, as uncomfortable as this is for most, the banking policies of the two states were similar. Henry Kelliher,

---

58   H W S Russell, The Duke of Bedford, *Propaganda for Proper Geese* (England, ca. 1939), 3-4. Bedford formed the British People's Party to campaign for peace and Social Credit, and the People's Campaign Against War and Usury. See: K Thomson, *'Hastings William Sackville Russell, The 12th Duke of Bedford & the Fight for Peace & Justice'*, Ab Aeterno, Issue no. 7, April-June 2011, (Academy of Social & Political Research), 40-43.

59   A Hitler, Reichstag speech, January 30, 1939. R de Roussy de Sales (ed.) op. cit., 457-458.

later knighted as 'Sir Henry', was a businessman, arts patron and served on the board of the Bank of New Zealand. He is known to New Zealanders primarily as the head of Dominion Breweries and as the initiator of the iconic milk-in-schools programme. Kelliher was also an avid campaigner for banking reform.[60] He was publisher of a home journal, *The Mirror*, a magazine that was head and shoulders intellectually above the plethora of current magazines for the 'liberated woman'. Kelliher's campaign for economic reform assisted the Labour Party in assuming Government.[61] Therefore, when consulting Kelliher's *Mirror* for a description of Germany's economic policies, we are looking at something other than a 'Nazi' propaganda sheet.

In 1938 *The Mirror* ran an article by its European correspondent, Bertram de Colonna, who wrote: 'Germany could not produce gold, but real wealth from land and forest, fields and factories. Labour was also available in plenty. In fact the unemployed totalled around seven million at the time'.[62] Capital was not available either domestically or internationally, and gold reserves were only sufficient to cover 10% of the currency in circulation. De Colonna writes that, 'The result was a decision by the government to issue and assume control of currency and credit'. One million marks of state credit were issued to finance public works including state housing. 'The bankers prophesied speedy bankruptcy. Those prophecies proved utterly wrong...' Newly created state banks issued state credit. 'The new money backed by the credit of the nation was gradually absorbed by the open money market'. This in turn brought a big increase in state revenue without the need for increasing taxation. Private banks were placed under state supervision and 'the rate of interest was limited by law'.

---

60 H J Kelliher, *New Zealand at the Cross-Roads* (Auckland, 1936).

61 Prime Minister Joseph Savage acknowledged the support of Kelliher in a 'Message to the People': 'I offer my congratulations and thanks to the Mirror for the monumental part that it played in laying the foundation of great economic changes for the benefit of the people, and trust that it will meet with deserving support in its progressive and fearless policy'. H J Kelliher ibid., between 56 and 57.

62 Bertram de Colonna, 'The Truth About Germany', *The Mirror*, Auckland, 1938.

De Colonna pointed out that the state money was in no way inflationary, (a frequent objection against such schemes by orthodox economists). The issue of credit and new money 'is based upon the actual production of real wealth', through greater industrial output. De Colonna stated that after five years of pursuing this policy it had proven its worth in keeping money in constant circulation, 'after all that is the only use of money – to circulate and exchange the wealth produced by the nation'.[63]

More recently a professional economist, Henry C K Liu[64], who can hardly be suspected of Hitlerism, analysed the methods by which Germany emerged from the Depression:

The Nazis came to power in Germany in 1933, at a time when its economy was in total collapse, with ruinous war-reparation obligations and zero prospects for foreign investment or credit. Yet through an independent monetary policy of sovereign credit and a full-employment public-works program, the Third Reich was able to turn a bankrupt Germany, stripped of overseas colonies it could exploit, into the strongest economy in Europe within four years, even before armament spending began. In fact, German economic recovery preceded and later enabled German rearmament, in contrast to the US economy, where constitutional roadblocks placed by the US Supreme Court on the New Deal delayed economic recovery until US entry to World War II put the US market economy on a war footing. While this observation is not an endorsement for Nazi philosophy, the effectiveness of German economic policy in this period, some of which had been started during the last phase of the Weimar Republic, is undeniable.[65]

---

63   Ibid.

64   Henry C K Liu is Chairman of the New York-based Liu Investment Group, and formerly a professor at the universities of California, Harvard and Columbia.

65   Henry C K Liu, 'Nazism and the German economic miracle', Asia Times Online, 24 May 2005, http://www.atimes.com/atimes/Global_Economy/GE24Dj01.html

Henry Liu adds an interesting comment regarding Communist China by way of comparison. It is instructive for us today in that Marxism has failed historically as an alternative to capitalism, especially with its inability to address the world financial system on which monopoly capitalism is based. Liu writes:

> After two and a half decades of economic reform toward neo-liberal market economy, China is still unable to accomplish in economic reconstruction what Nazi Germany managed in four years after coming to power, i.e., full employment with a vibrant economy financed with sovereign credit without the need to export, which would challenge that of Britain, the then superpower. This is because China made the mistake of relying on foreign investment instead of using its own sovereign credit.[66]

Autarky

The aim of National Socialist economic policy was to make Germany *autarkic* – self-sufficient[67] – and not reliant on the vagaries of word trade and foreign loan capital. Germany was freed from international debt. Historian Richard Overy states:

> Among the first acts of the new government were the repudiation of further [war] reparations payments and the reduction or suspension of repayments on foreign loans. Almost no new loans were taken up, while existing loans from the 1920s were reduced substantially because of the willingness of foreign bondholders to dump their German stock once interest payments had been blocked. The bonds were bought back at rock-bottom prices by agents secretly working for the German government. By 1939 only 15 percent of the foreign debt outstanding in 1932 still

---

66   Ibid.

67   Richard Overy, *The Dictators: Hitler's Germany and Stalin's Russia* (London: Allen Lane, 2004) 418-419.

remained in foreign hands. The foreign capital relied on in the 1920s was replaced by capital supplied by the German state, whose debt trebled between 1933 and 1939.[68]

While Overy goes into considerable detail about Germany's economic planning, nothing is mentioned in regard to the foundation of that planning; namely state credit. Overy states also that 'trade was increasingly arranged on a bilateral barter basis...'[69] Another interesting aspect is that of 'The Dividend Law of 1934' which restricted profits and dividends to no more than 6 per cent, and required enterprises to reinvest any surplus or forfeit it to the state. Capital could not be freely transferred abroad, and its use within Germany was restricted by the Supervisory Office for Credit Affairs (set up in December 1934) so that it might be directed to specific national tasks rather than to the most profitable.[70]

Utilisation of Profits

It is hence a fallacy to claim – as do both Marxists and Libertarians – that Germany (1933-45) was a bastion of monopoly-capital and that the big industrialists controlled Hitler.[71] Whatever Germany undertook in its persecutions, totalitarianism and wars, the fact remains that in the background looms the suppressed economic miracle that was achieved by using similar methods to those used on a more limited scale by the First New Zealand Labour Government, and others. If the Third Reich era of German history could be studied with objectivity we might find an answer to the global debt crisis, or might have avoided any such crisis in the first place. Indeed, if it was not for wartime hysteria, which has yet to relent nearly seventy years after the war's end, we might have utilised 'Nazi' discoveries on the

---

68   Ibid., 420.

69   Ibid.

70   Ibid., 439.

71   Cf. Antony Sutton, *Wall Street and the Rise of Hitler* (Suffolk: Bloomfield Books, 1976).

relationship between tobacco and cancer, instead of the tobacco industry being permitted to bury such evidence until recently,[72] just as the USA and USSR utilised 'Nazi' discoveries on rocket propulsion.

Japan

What is even less known is that in 1929 Maj. C H Douglas went to Tokyo to deliver a paper to an international engineering conference, entitled 'The Application of Engineering Methods to Finance'. Some of Douglas' books on Social Credit were translated into Japanese and there developed considerable interest in banking reform. Eric Butler, long time advocate of Social Credit in Australia, related that many representatives of the Japanese Government subscribed to Social Credit journals, such as the Australian journal, *The New Times*.[73]

The Bank of Japan, formed in 1882, had from its start the Imperial House as the major shareholder. However in 1932 it was reorganised specifically as a state bank. Stephen M Goodson, a financial consultant, founder of the Abolition of Income Tax and Usury Party, and a former director on the board of South Africa's Reserve Bank, has stated of the Japanese banking system:

> The reform of the central bank was completed in February 1942 when the Bank of Japan Law as remodelled on the Reichsbank Act of Germany of 1939. Credit would be issued by the bank as the interests and productivity of Japan required.

> During the period 1931-41 manufacturing output and industrial production increased by 140% and 136% respectively, while national income and Gross National Product (GNP) were up

---

72 Robert N Proctor, *The Nazi War on Cancer* (New Jersey: Princeton University Press, 1999).

73 Eric D Butler, *The Truth About the Australian League of Rights* (Melbourne: Heritage Publications 1985), 9.

by 241% and 259% respectively. These remarkable increases exceeded by a wide margin the economic growth of the rest of the industrialized world. In the labour market unemployment declined from 5.3% in 1930 to 3.0% in 1938. Industrial disputes decreased with the number of stoppages down from 998 in 1931 to 159 in 1941.[74]

Again, Japan's achievements in the economic sector have been obscured by focusing entirely on wartime Nippon.

Fascist Italy

Mussolini had for nearly the first decade of the Fascist regime pursued a pragmatic policy that included a free market economy, while simultaneously building the Corporatist State, but crucially already by 1926 had intervened in the banking sector. Italian Fascism sought primarily to create an autarchic state not subject to the vagaries of world trade and finance, and was open to any system in the pursuit of such a goal. Because the regime did not implement a policy of nationalisation of industry in the Marxist sense, historians and economists simplistically claim that Fascism served the interests of Capital in suppressing Labour.

By 1931 the regime was ready to implement a new fiscal policy. That year the State assumed supervision over the major banks via the Instituto Mobiliare Italiano (IMI). However, already in 1926 the Bank of Italy had been given jurisdiction over all banking and the issue of bank notes, and a minimum reserve of capital was required, including a minimum gold reserve. During this period the Bank was brought under direction of the State.[75] New banks had to be approved by the Ministry of Finance, in consultation with the Bank of Italy.[76]

---

74 Stephen M Goodson, 'Why the USA forced the Empire of Japan into World War II', Abolition of Usury and Taxation Party. http://www.aitup.org.za/

75 *The Bank of Italy from its inception to the 1936 Banking Law*', 'The post-war years and the consolidation of the Bank's public role', Banca D'Italia, http://www.bancaditalia.it/ bancaditalia/storia/1936/il_dopoguerra

76 David A Alhadeff, *Competition and Controls in Banking: A Study of the Regulation of*

In 1936 the Bank of Italy and the major banks became public institutions, under the Banking Law, making the Bank of Italy the sole agency for advancing credit to other banks. Limits on State borrowing from the Bank of Italy were eliminated, and Italy was taken off the gold standard.[77] Alhadeff states of the 1936 Act:

> The controls established over the banks by the 1926 law were a prelude to the much broader range of controls authorized by the Banking Law of 1936. The 1926 law had regulated the collection of savings to protect depositors. The 1936 law went further and declared that 'the collection of savings from the public in whatever form and the exercise of credit activities are functions of public interest...'[78] To implement this view, a comprehensive system of bank controls was established. ... [79]

The Instituto per la Ricostruzione Industriale (IRI), was set up in January 1933 as a holding company to control major industrial corporations in which the State had purchased controlling stock.[80]

Fascist Italy had thus gone a long way towards harnessing the productivity of the nation for the benefit of the commonwealth. Italian Fascism sought to complete this process of 'socialisation' under the radical programme devised by former leading Italian Communist theorist Nicola Bombacci, who saw Fascism as a more genuinely anti-Capitalist doctrine than Marxism, in the short-lived Fascist redoubt of the Italian Social Republic (1943-

Bank Competition in Italy, France, and England (University of California Pres, 1968), 25.

77   'The Depression and the 1936 Banking Law', Banca D'Italia, op. cit., http://www.bancaditalia.it/bancaditalia/storia/1936/la_depressione

78   Article 1, Royal Decree Law, 12 March 1936.

79   David A Alhadeff, op. cit., 25.

80   Alexander J De Grand, *Fascist Italy and Nazi Germany: The 'Fascist' Style of Rule* (London: Routledge, 2004), 52.

1945).[81] The ultimate vision of this 'Republican Fascism' was the creation of a united Europe which included 'Abolition of the internal Capitalist system and resolute struggle against the Plutocracies'.[82] On the economic question, the *Verona Manifest*, the founding programme of the Social Republic, promulgated the co-management and profit-sharing of employees in industry,[83] within the Corporate State structure of Fascism that united all class interests into a unitary social organism. The co-management and profit-sharing basis of the Social Republic was detailed in the 'Companies' Socialisation Bill of Law'.[84] The Social Republic was a bold attempt to create a new social order, very much in keeping with Pope Leo XIII Encyclical *Rerum Novarum* (1891), that had inspired a variety of movements for social justice across the world, seeking answers to the materialist hydra of Marxism and Capitalism, from Belloc and Chesterton's 'Distributist' movement in Britain to Father Coughlin's Social Justice movement in the USA, to Dollfuss' Austria[85] and Salazar's Portuguese 'New State'.[86]

Lincoln and Kennedy

US President Abraham Lincoln had recourse to the issuing of the Greenbacks during the Civil War. Lincoln attempted to circumvent the private banking system and initially issued $150,000,000 interest-free '*Lincoln Greenbacks*' directly through the US Treasury to fund the war. However such interest-free state credit was superseded by the National Banking Act 1863, which authorised the issue of Interest Bearing and Compound Interest Treasury Notes. The Federal Reserve Bank Act of 1913 authorised the establishment of a central bank that would issue credit based on usury.

---

81   Erik Norling, *Revolutionary Fascism* (Lisbon, Finis Mundi Press, 2011).

82   Verona Manifest, point 8 (b) 15 November 1943, cited by Norling, ibid., 68.

83   Ibid., point 12.

84   Norling, ibid., 105-116.

85   Fr. Johannes Messner, *Dollfuss: An Austrian Patriot* (Norfolk, Virginia, Gates of Vienna Books, 2004).

86   F C C Egerton, *Salazar: Builder of Portugal* (London: Hodder and Stoughton, 1943).

In 1963 President John F Kennedy attempted to circumvent the private bankers by 'Executive Order 11110', which bypassed the Federal Reserve System and authorised US Treasury to issue $4,000,000,000 of 'United States Notes'; interest and debt free, used to fund new production, which were withdrawn from circulation at the rate of the consumption of production.[87]

Muslim Banking

Muslim banking practise remains an anomaly in the world financial system, since the *Quran* prohibits usury. The *Quran* states: 'Those who eat Riba [usury] will not stand except like the standing of a person beaten by Shaitan leading him to insanity'.[88] This is not dissimilar to the Biblical dictums upheld for centuries by the Catholic Church. For example, amongst the numerous papal edicts on usury, on the 1st November 1745 Pope Benedict XIV stated: 'One cannot condone the sin of usury'.

Islamic states under Islamic law prohibit non-productive economic activity. That is, economic parasitism is actually outlawed by religious sanction, as it once was in Western Christendom. Now that there has been another crisis in the debt-finance system, even Western financial institutions are looking at Islamic banking practice. Westpac Banking Corporation for example has sought involvement with Islamic banking by 'offering a commodity-trading facility aimed at overseas investors that operates under the principles of Islamic law'.

Since Islamic finance prohibits the earning of interest there is instead a focus on profit-sharing based on buying and selling tangible assets such as property. A news report said of this:

> The move by Westpac coincides with an Australian federal government attempt to promote involvement in Islamic financing. The Trade Minister, Simon Crean, launched

---

87   John F Kennedy, Executive Order No. 11110, 4 June 1963.

88   *Quran*, al-Baqarah (The Cow).

a study outlining opportunities for the financial services sector to tap into the sharia-compliant investment and banking markets. This followed the recommendation last month by a government-backed finance taskforce to overhaul tax rules to ensure Islamic financing products receive equal treatment. The Australian Financial Centre Forum, which released a broader report into the nation's finance sector, highlighted Islamic financing as a potential funding source for the nation's banks. The market for Islamic financial services has grown rapidly in recent years, it is estimated to be close to $1 trillion.[89]

How ironic that parasitic finance should now turn in desperation to the hated Muslims and their anti-parasitical system of finance - that the parasite might feed from another host. Hopefully the Muslims will heed the old adage, to paraphrase: 'He who sups with Shaitan should use a long spoon.'

---

89   E Johnston, (2010): 'Westpac trade deal courts Islamic investors,' *Sydney Morning Herald*, 13 February, 2010, http://www.stuff.co.nz/business/industries/banking-finance/3323205/Westpac-trade-deal-courts-Islamic-investors

Playing Cards Saved Quebec

Orthodox economists and those with vested interests in maintaining the financial status quo claim that any system other than that devised by them, which of necessity is based around debt finance – usury – is unworkable, crackpot, and inflationary, and can only end in disaster. This fiction can only be maintained by the widespread ignorance of history, in regard to the manner by which communities and entire states have been salvaged from ruin by innovative financial alternatives, which we have been considering herein. While our parents and grandparents knew a lot more and they widely discussed the banking system, there is little evidence of a present day awakening on economic realities despite the colossal debt that is catching up to most of the world.

During the Depression era, there was widespread demand for banking reform. This awareness was greatly assisted in the British Commonwealth states by the tour of Maj. C H Douglas. Other countries had their advocates for monetary reform aiming to replace the debt finance system, as we have seen. Such things are now forgotten history. Few realise that Guernsey Island saved itself from destitution in 1820 by issuing its own currency, which is still used, independently of British Stirling; that not only did Lincoln issue 'Greenbacks' during the Civil War, bypassing the debt finance system, but that the Confederacy also issued Graybacks as 'non-interest bearing money [which] remained the predominant medium of exchange',[1] and that President John Kennedy did something similar with the issue of US Notes via the US Treasury, bypassing the Federal Reserve Bank system.

---

1   Marc Weidenmeir, '*Money and Finance in the Confederate States of America*', E H Net, http://eh.net/encyclopedia/article/weidenmier.finance.confederacy.is

A Successful Gamble

While today's monetary reformers are generally aware that the Bank of Canada issued over half of Canada's credit during 1935-1945 and up to 30% until the mid 1970s,[2] an earlier example of debt-free currency that is unlikely to be as widely known is the manner by which French Canada was saved from destitution in 1685.

French Canada (Quebec) was dependent on an annual remittance from Paris. In 1685 King Louis XIV failed to provide French Canada with its financial sustenance. Fortunately the 'Intendant' of the Province, M de Meulle, had not been blessed with an education into the necessities of orthodox economics as it then was and remains today; of such panaceas as 'balancing the budget', 'belt tightening' or increasing taxes. Simple man as he obviously was, he apparently did not understand that money and credit are only supposed to appear when loaned into circulation as a usurious debt. So instead of disbanding his troops, whom he could not pay, and making redundancies in his public service, thereby obliging employers to lay off workers due to the lack of purchasing power, de Meulle thought that since money was not available from France he would simply make his own.

Without even a printing press to produce a currency, he called in all the decks of playing cards that could be gathered, and cut them into quarters. On these he wrote the value that each was to represent, gained public confidence in their efficacy as legal tender by giving them his personal guarantee, and spent them into circulation.

While the Mother Country was broke and in such debt as to be a major precipitant of the Revolution a century later, French

---

2   H Chorney, Associate Professor of Political Economy and Public Policy, Concordia University, Montreal; J Hotson, Professor of Economics, University of Waterloo; Mario Seccareccia, Assoc. Professor of Economics, University of Ottawa; 'The Deficit Made Me Do It!', Introduction, CCPA Popular Economics Series, Editor: Ed Finn, Canadian Centre For Policy Alternatives, 2010. http://lists.topica.com/lists/VOW/read/message. html?mid=813781210&sort=d&start=6327

Canada maintained itself. M de Meulle reported to the Minister in Paris:

My Lord - I have found myself this year in great straits with regard to the subsistence of the soldiers. You did not provide for funds, My Lord, until January last. I have, notwithstanding, kept them in provisions until September, which makes eight full months. I have drawn from my own funds and from those of my friends, all I have been able to get, but at last finding them without means to render me further assistance, and not knowing to what saint to pay my vows, money being extremely scarce, having distributed considerable sums on every side for the pay of the soldiers, it occurred to me to issue, instead of money, notes on [playing] cards, which I have had cut in quarters. I send you My Lord, the three kinds, one is for four francs, another for forty sols, and the third for fifteen sols, because with these three kinds, I was able to make their exact pay for one month. I have issued an ordinance by which I have obliged all the inhabitants to receive this money in payments, and to give it circulation, at the same time pledging myself, in my own name, to redeem the said notes. No person has refused them, and so good has been the effect that by this means the troops have lived as usual. There were some merchants who, privately, had offered me money at the local rate on condition that I would repay them in money at the local rate in France, to which I could not consent as the King would have lost a third; that is, for 10,000 he would have paid 40,000 livres; thus personally, by my credit and by my management, I have saved His Majesty 13,000 livres.

De Meulle, Quebec,
24th September, 1685.[3]

---

3   *Canadian Currency, Exchange and Finance During the French Period*, Vol. 1, ed. Adam Shortt (New York: Burt Franklin, Research Source Works Series no. 235, 1968).

Six years later there was another shortage of money, and again the playing card currency was issued. According to Sir Ralph Norman Angell, Nobel Laureate and British Member of Parliament, the currency became 'exceedingly popular and remained current during the whole of the remainder of that century and the first half of the next'.[4] As late as 1749 ordinances were passed in French Canada increasing the issue to a million livres. A N Field, a well-known expert on monetary reform in New Zealand during the Depression era, commented:

> What M de Meulle did was a very simple thing. At the same time it was a very profound thing. M de Meulle probably never considered that there was anything very profound about it. It was just an obvious, commonsense step; and it was the right step. Money is merely a ticket entitling the bearer to goods and services, and it matters little whether it is made of gold or cut out playing cards.[5]

Field concluded with a lesson just as applicable today as it was when he wrote in 1931, stating that

> The steps that were taken by M de Meulle in Canada in 1685 could be taken by the Parliament of New Zealand tomorrow if it wished... Parliament does not take any such step because it is the slave of false ideas, false ideas that are strangling and choking our civilisation. Because of these ideas we remain in a stupid slump that we could walk out of it we chose. [6]

And if the King's grandson, Louis XVI, had used his head a century later, and had undertaken a method as simple but as effective as M de Meulle's, he might not have lost it, and history might have taken a far different course than that of the bloodied vista opened up by the French Revolution.

---

4   R N Angell, *The Story of Money* (London: 1929) cited by A N Field, 'The Next Best Thing: Paper Money Better than No Money', *God's Own Country (And the Devil's Own Mess)*, Nelson, 1931, No. 1, 3.

5   A N Field, ibid.

6   Ibid., p. 4.

'Graybacks' & the Confederacy

The goodwill towards the Southern states that one might expect from monetary reformers has been clouded by the claim that the War of Secession was instigated by international bankers for the control of the USA, and specifically that it was the South that was for this purpose backed by the Rothschilds and other European banking dynasties in Europe. While monetary reformers often allude to Abraham Lincoln having issued state credit in the form of the 'Greenbacks', and therefore Lincoln has become something of an icon among those who advocate alternatives to the usurious financial system, seldom realised is that the Confederacy issued its own 'Graybacks', and did not have any type of fellowship with international finance. The condemnation of the South often includes an anti-Semitic element, because the Confederate Secretary of State, Judah P Benjamin, was Jewish, and from there flights of fancy roam free, including the claim that Benjamin was a 'Rothschild agent' and even that he was a 'Rothschild relative'.

The 'Grayback' served the Confederacy as the 'Greenback' served the Union, and perhaps moreso, as the Confederacy was shut out of financial markets. It was a pragmatic move, and one that better served the Confederate States of America (CSA) by force of circumstances than going cap-in-hand to the international money-lenders. Hence, the 'Grayback' is an example of state credit used on a wide scale that allowed the functioning of an economy without recourse to usurious debt, and stands with other examples such as the use of Reserve Bank state credit by the 1935 New Zealand Labour Government. Given the present widespread economic tumult caused by the compound interest intrinsic to the debt-finance system that controls much of the world, a consideration of alternative systems of banking and finance are of vital importance, but are now problems that are seldom understood by the 'Right'. This was not always the case, as exemplified by examples given here.

Was the Confederacy a Rothschild Tool?

One of the first, if not the first, to circulate the allegation that the Confederacy was controlled by the Rothschilds as a means of weakening the Union was the Czarist émigré Count Cherep-Spiridovitch, who cites an alleged interview with German Chancellor Bismarck in 1876:

> The division of the United States into two federations of equal force was decided long before the civil war by the High Financial Power of Europe. These bankers were afraid that the United States, if they remained in one block and as one nation, would attain economical and financial independence, which would upset the financial domination over the world. The voice of the Rothschilds predominated. They foresaw tremendous booty if they could substitute two feeble democracies indebted to the Jewish financiers for the vigorous republic confident and self-providing. Therefore they started their emissaries in order to exploit the question of slavery and thus to dig an abyss between the two parts of the republic....[1]

The alleged quote from Bismarck goes on to praise Lincoln for being conscious of the plans of the 'Jewish financiers' and for bypassing them with his own credit, for which he was assassinated.

The Czarist Count's interest in this matter might be accounted for by:

---

[1] Maj. Gen. Count Cherep-Spiridovich, *The Secret World Government* (New York: the Anti-Bolshevist Publishing Association, 1926), 180. The alleged quote was published in *La Vieille France*, N-216, March 1921, according to Cherep-Spiridovich.

His tendency, common among Czarist émigrés in the aftermath of the Bolshevik Revolution, where Jewish involvement was conspicuousness, to seek out explanations for all upheavals by tracing their origins to the Jews. The Count's book *The Secret World Government*, ascribes much of history to the 'hidden hand' of Jewry. The Count sees the same 'hidden hand' that killed Czar Nicholas and his family after the Bolshevik seizure, as being that which also assassinated Lincoln.[2]

There is a certain plausibility to the latter contention regarding Czar Nicholas I being brought down because of Russia's sovereignty from international finance capital. This will be considered in the following chapter.

The historically good relations that had existed between the United States and Czarist Russia, Cherep-Spiridovitch alludes to Russia being 'friendly to the Union cause and in 1863, when the success of the cause looked doubtful, a fleet of Russian war ships came into the harbor in New York'.[3] Cherep-Spiridovitch states that Czar Alexander II's orders were for the Russian fleet to be ready to 'take orders from Lincoln'.[4]

These accounts have been repeated ever since, especially among Right-wing conspiracy theorists, but are incorrect. The circumstances of the Russian Atlantic Fleet's entry into New York harbour are related by Marshall B Davidson, who captures the imagery of welcome and jubilation among New Yorkers at the arrival of the Russians. Davidson states that at the time there were many rumours as to why the Russians had arrived, chief among them being that they were there to assist the Union against the South:

2   Ibid., 181.

3   Ibid.

4   Ibid.

…In any case, New York seems generally to have assumed that this was a 'friendship visit', and must indicate Russian support for the Northern cause – a legend that lost nothing in its retelling, over the years, and that was not finally put to rest until 1915.[5]

The reference by Davidson that the matter was 'finally put to rest' in 1915 is optimistic as the legend has remained firm among certain quarters, Cherep-Spiridovitch's 1926 book being one such example. Marshall states that at the time the Russian ships sailed into New York and San Francisco, a potential for conflict had emerged between Russia and England, Austria and France over Russia's suppression of the Polish revolt. In 1915 Dr Frank A Golder, having had access to official Russian records, wrote in the *American Historical Review* that the Russian visits were not ones of 'friendship', but had been highly secret manoeuvres to get the best of the Russian ships into safe ports, the concern being that they would be trapped in the event of conflict with the European powers.[6] New York and San Francisco were the only convenient ports for the best ships of Russia's Atlantic and Pacific fleets. From here the Russian ships could harass British commercial routes. The manoeuvre seems to have succeeded, states Davidson, as there was no ultimatum against Russia. 'That they came as interested supporters of the Northern cause was a notion concocted and nurtured by the Unionists who were only too happy to imagine it to be true', writes Davidson.[7]

However, ninety-five years on from the article by Dr Golder, and the image of an alliance between Lincoln and Czar Alexander against 'international financiers' and/or the Jewish 'hidden hand' is still being nurtured. While those with what one might call a cynical attitude towards Jews see Confederate Secretary

---

5   Marshall B Davidson, 'A Royal Welcome for the Russian Navy', *America and Russia: a century and a half of dramatic encounters*, edited by Oliver Jensen (New York: Simon and Schuster, 1962), 64.

6   Ibid., 69.

7   Ibid., 70.

of State Judah P Benjamin as sufficient reason to consider the Confederacy as nothing but a Rothschild contrivance, monetary reformers see Lincoln in heroic terms for his having issued Greenbacks as state credit. What is overlooked is that the Confederacy issued its own Greenback equivalent, known as Graybacks. Hence the scenario is that, for example, according to Rochelle Ascher, a supporter of American economist and 'conspiracy theorist' Lyndon LaRouche, Lincoln fought the 'British-backed New York banking system' bringing banking under control and issuing $450 million state created Greenbacks to fund the war.[8]

The very fact that the Confederacy was not supported by international finance prompted the necessity of the Confederacy to generate its own credit. While it might seem that the Grayback state credit issue caused inflation and thereby confirms that objections to state credit, what should be noted is that price-inflation was caused by large-scale counterfeiting of Graybacks from the North, and was also affected greatly according to public confidence or loss of confidence according to the course of the war. State currency amounted to 60% of the Confederate States of America (CSA) revenue during the war.[9] Marc Wiedenmier states that the money issued by the CSA was interest-free:

> Non-interest-bearing money remained the predominant medium of exchange in the Southern Confederacy despite the existence of large quantities of interest-bearing money.... state and Confederate governments forced banks to accept both types of money through *de facto* legal restrictions.[10]

The diehard manner by which myths about the Confederacy persist is accounted for by the presence of Judah P Benjamin,

---

8   Rochelle Ascher, 'The Lessons of Abraham Lincoln', *American Almanac*, 1992, http://american_almanac.tripod.com/ascher1.htm

9   Marc Weidenmier, op. cit.

10   Ibid.

more than by any other factor. Such a 'Court Jew' (sic) can only be explained, so the story goes, by the existence of a high-powered conspiracy that placed him in that position. We have previously seen how this attitude was taken up by the Czarist émigré Count Cherep-Spiridovitch, in 1926. The White Russian émigrés were to become very influential in shaping 'anti-Semitic' ideologies outside Russia. Two obvious examples are Alfred Rosenberg who was to have a major input into the ideology of the National Socialist party in Germany; and Boris Brasol, a Czarist jurist who had been a member of a Russian trade delegation in the USA when the Russian revolutions destroyed his world, who maintained influential contacts and was instrumental in popularising the *Protocols of Zion* in the USA. At any rate, the anti-Southern attitude was taken up by leading American conservatives whom one might normally expect would support the aristocratic and agrarian virtues and states' rights of the South against Northern industrialism and plutocracy, and might have done so if it was not for the pervasive bugbear of Judah P Benjamin.

One of the most prominent of the American conservatives was Gerald L K Smith, a force in his day first as aide to Louisiana's Senator Huey Long, then as an eloquent 'America Firster' along with Father Coughlin, Charles Lindbergh et al., campaigning to keep the USA out of the war in Europe.[11] During the course of his long career attacking Communism, Zionism and Judaism, including what he states was his campaign in the South that was instrumental in the creation of the 'Dixie Party',[12]Smith published an article on the War of Secession in which he stated that:

...if we look behind the scenes we will find that the 'slave question' was but the surface issue. Below the surface ran

---

11   Gerald L K Smith, *Besieged Patriot: Autobiographical Episodes Exposing Communism, Traitorism and Zionism* (Eureka Springs, Arkansas: Christian Nationalist Crusade, 1978).

12   Ibid., 37.

a current of intrigue that ended with the assassination of Abraham Lincoln because he was determined that the United States be free from the bondage of the international bankers.[13]

Smith cites a passage from a book by John Reeves, who was said to have had access to the Rothschild archives, in which Reeves states that the division of the USA was decided by the Rothschilds at the wedding of Leonara, daughter of Lionel, to her cousin, Alphonse, son of James of Paris, at the family gathering in the City of London, 1857. British Prime Minister Disraeli is reported to have said that it was here that a plan was devised to divide the USA into two, split between James and Lionel.[14]

Be that as it may, Smith jumped to the conclusion that, 'Judah P Benjamin was chosen by the Rothschilds to do their work in the United States and he was the first adviser to Jefferson Davis, the President of the Southern Confederacy...'[15] The claim is repeated that Czar Alexander knew of the Rothschild plans for the USA and that this was the reason for his dispatching ships to New York and San Francisco harbours. The article concludes with the often-used alleged material from Bismarck. Other articles attempting to relate the Confederacy to Rothschild domination follow the same pattern to the present time.

Judah P Benjamin: Davis' 'Court Jew'?

As indicated by the several references above, the CSA's alleged subservience to Rothschild interests centres around Judah P Benjamin, Confederate Secretary of State, who is called by friend and foe alike the 'brains of the Confederacy'.[16]

---

13   Gerald L K Smith, 'Abraham Lincoln and the Rothschilds: Civil War was not fought over slavery but financial freedom', *The Cross and the Flag*, Arkansas, June, 1971. Also published as a leaflet.

14   Smith, ibid., citing John Reeves, *The Rothschilds: the financial rulers of nations*, 228.

15   Ibid.

16   '*The Brains of the Confederacy*', Jewish-American History Foundation, http://www. jewish-history.com/civilwar/judahpb.html

Benjamin has been described not only as a 'Rothschild agent', but also as a 'Rothschild relative'. Benjamin's association with Rothschild agencies is said to have started early in his career. The LaRouche sponsored 'Modern History Project', which sees the conspiratorial apparatus as of Anglo-imperialist[17] rather than Jewish pedigree, for example, states:

> Judah P Benjamin (1811-84) of the law firm of Slidell, Benjamin and Conrad in Louisiana was a Rothschild agent who became Secretary of State for the Confederacy in 1862. His law partner John Slidell (August Belmont's[18] wife's uncle) was the Confederate envoy to France. Slidell's daughter was married to Baron Frederick d'Erlanger in Frankfurt who was related to the Rothschilds and acted on their behalf. Slidell was the representative of the South who borrowed money from the d'Erlangers to finance the Confederacy.[19]

The Canadian conspiracy theorist Commander William Guy Carr wrote without evidence or references that, 'Judah P Benjamin, a Rothschild relative, was appointed as their professional strategist in America'.[20] There does not appear to be any evidence or reason for believing that Benjamin was a 'relative of the Rothschilds'.

The attitude of Rothschild's actual agent in the USA, August Belmont, who was also National Chairman of the Democratic Party, was however, avidly, fanatically pro-Union. The attitude

---

17 For a repudiation of the also widely held view that the international financial system is largely under the heel of British neo-imperialism, stemming from the Round Table Groups of Cecil Rhodes and Alfred Milner, see: K R Bolton, 'Don't blame the Brits: is there an Anglophile conspiracy seeking world domination?', *Foreign Policy Journal*, August 8, 2010 <http://www.foreignpolicyjournal.com/2010/08/08/dont-blame-the-brits/>

18 August Belmont was Rothschild emissary for the Northern states.

19 The Modern History Project, Chapter 2.1 'The Bank of the US', http://www. modernhistoryproject.org/mhp/ArticleDisplay.php?Article=FinalWarn02-1 The claim that Slidell arranged the Erlanger loan is incorrect.

20 William Guy Carr, *Pawns in the Game* (California: Angriff Press, n.d.) 53.

of the Rothschilds towards either side was cautious, but Belmont warned that if it were not Rothschild funding that was provided to the North, which Belmont was convinced would win any conflict, the Rothschilds' rivals would take their place. The bankers who did emerge best from the war were J and W Seligman and Company who, 'had been the main financial stay of Lincoln's administration during the war and they reaped the benefits afterward'.[21]

Diplomatic Failures With Europe

While it is generally held by friend and foe alike that Rothschilds reigned above all in Europe, logic would suggest that Britain, France and other states heavily influenced by Rothschild lending, would be inclined towards formal support for the Confederacy, if the CSA was a client state of the bankers. This was not the case, despite much being made of supposedly pro-South sentiments among some quarters in England and France.

Despite Benjamin's efforts, diplomatic recognition by Britain was not forthcoming. Moreover, in 1863 Benjamin closed the CSA mission to England, and evicted the remaining British consular agents from the South.[22] This latter expulsion was at the direct instigation of Benjamin when he called a Cabinet meeting while Davis was *en route* to Tennessee, an action that nonetheless brought prompt agreement from Davis.[23] Efforts to secure French recognition were also unsuccessful. Indeed, in a breach of supposed British neutrality, by 1863 around 75,000 Irishmen had volunteered to fight with the North, as did Germans and other foreign recruits.[24]

---

21   Derek Wilson, *Rothschild: the story of wealth and power* (London: André Deutsch, 1988), 188.

22   Albert N Rosen, op.cit., 294.

23   Ibid.

24   Robert Douthat Meade and William C Davis, op.cit., 296.

Loans Not Forthcoming

As mentioned above, Seligman provided the North with its financial wherewithal, despite the claim that the Union stood against international finance, while the South was in thrall to usury.

The primary claim in regard to the 'Rothschild' (sic) funding of the Confederacy is that an important loan was secured from the Erlanger bank in Paris. This financial arrangement was not however favourable to the Confederacy; it was nothing other than a typical money-lending deal that did the South no favours.

Much is made of CSA emissary and Benjamin's former law partner John Slidell's daughter being engaged to Baron Erlanger; and Slidell's niece being married to August Belmont, the Rothschild representative to the Northern States.[25] Despite the family connections, the Erlangers did not show the Confederacy any support outside of a single usurious business deal. Benjamin personally negotiated the $2.5 million loan with Baron Emile Erlanger when the latter visited Richmond, Virginia. Benjamin hoped that involvement with the banking house of Erlanger and Cie, and with the Erlanger family, who were close friends and advisors to Emperor Louis Napoleon, would secure diplomatic relations with France,[26] having failed to make any headway with Britain. The original plan had been for a loan of $25 million to be repaid with bonds and the sale of cotton, with the Erlangers reaping a huge profit of 23% commission and 8% for handling the bonds.[27] Ironically, it was Benjamin who regarded the terms with outrage, as 'usury'. Intensive face-to-face negotiations by Benjamin with Erlanger reduced the rate from 8% to 7%. Speculators and investors in Europe bought up the bonds and the Erlangers made a quick profit.[28]

---

25   Robert N Rosen, op.cit., 79.

26   Ibid.

27   Ibid.

28   Ibid.

The seminal study on funding and diplomacy during the American Civil War is Jay Sexton's[29] *Debtor Diplomacy.*[30] Sexton does not try to obfuscate the role of international finance in politics. He states that the desire of the American states to gain European capital influenced foreign policy, and that the primary influence was that of Britain, and this influence was particularly evident during the Civil War. 'Furthermore, the financial needs of the United States (and the Confederacy) imparted significant political power to an elite group of London-based financiers who became intimately involved in American foreign relations during this period',[31] which Sexton describes as: 'The unprecedented power of an elite group of international financiers'.[32]

The mid-nineteenth century witnessed the great British-based banking houses reach the pinnacle of their power and influence in American affairs. Led by Baring Brothers, the Rothschilds, and George Peabody and Company (the predecessor to the house of J P Morgan), banks in the City of London were the architects of nearly every facet of the Atlantic economy. In addition to negotiating loans and marketing American securities abroad, banks such as the Barings and Rothschilds underwrote transatlantic trade, provided insurance, exchanged currencies, and compiled influential market reports. During the westward flow of capital across the Atlantic, however, it remained the central function of the leading transatlantic banks. Ninety percent of the United States' foreign indebtness in 1861 was of British origin.[33]

The financial and commercial power of these banks 'extended to them significant political and diplomatic influence on both sides

---

29   Oxford University Lecturer in American History.

30   Jay Sexton, *Debtor Finance: Finance and American Foreign Relations in the Civil War Era 1837-1873* (New York: Oxford University Press, 2005).

31   Ibid., 1.

32   Ibid., 12.

33   Ibid.

of the Atlantic', adds Sexton, and he alludes to the poem 'Don Juan' by Lord Byron, where it is stated that the Barings and the Rothschilds are the 'true lords of Europe'.[34]

In the USA these bankers also exercised considerable influence through the connections of their emissaries; in particular August Belmont, and Thomas Ward and Daniel Webster acting for Barings, in Massachusetts, whom Sexton describes as 'highly influential politicians and lobbyists'.[35] "These international banks established a network of high finance and high politics that connected Britain and the United States and merged international finance with international relations."[36]

Hence, Sexton confirms what so-called 'conspiracy theorists' are often scoffed at for by academe and media; that there was – and is – an international elite of bankers who wield political power through their use of credit and trade. This is also how the eminent historian, Dr Carroll Quigley of Harvard, described these same international bankers when he wrote that they are, 'devoted to secrecy and the secret use of financial influence on political life'.[37] Quigley described their aim as being:

> To form a single financial system on an international scale which manipulated the quantity and flow of money so that they were able to influence, if not control, governments on one side and industries on the other. The men who did this aspired to establish dynasties of international bankers and were at least as successful at this as were many of the dynastic political rulers.[38]

Amidst the power of the financial elite over much of Europe and the North, the most that can be said for CSA relations with

---

34   Ibid.

35   Ibid., 13.

36   Ibid.

37   Carroll Quigley, op. cit., 52.

38   Ibid., p. 51.

the supposedly pro-Confederate England is that Confederate emissaries secured Enfield rifles from the London Armoury, which also provided arms for the North.[39]

The only bank that was sympathetic to the Confederacy was Fraser, Trenholm and Company, Liverpool, under the directorship of Charles Prioleau, which became the Confederacy's 'unofficial bank'. This hardly amounts to collusion between international finance and the Confederacy, let alone with the Rothschilds. Sexton observes, 'the bank was far from a financial powerhouse by most estimations', but by 1860 had become a leading cotton importer.[40] Charles Prioleau was a South Carolinian, 'who had long attempted to free the South from, as he viewed it, the economic hegemony of the North'.[41] Hence the motivation of the firm, headed by a Southerner, was not only one of Confederate sympathies but that the primary individual concerned, Prioleau, wanted to assist the South in opposing the plutocratic interests centred in the North. The company was responsible for arranging the ships that ran the Northern blockade, and its own ships even flew the Confederate Flag. In 1861 CSA President Jefferson Davis authorized the use of the bank as the Confederacy's depository.[42] However, the agency of this relatively modest bank could not compensate for the lack of credit from international finance, and already by 1862 the CSA's account with Fraser, Trenholm was in severe overdraft.

Considering the disruption of the cotton trade to England as the result of war what is remarkable is the lack of support that Britain showed the Confederacy, despite turning a blind eye to the supply of ships from Britain. What the international financiers of The City of London sought by 1862 was a quick diplomatic solution to the war. However, Sexton emphasises that:

---

39   Jay Sexton, op.cit., 142.

40   Ibid., 144.

41   Ibid..

42   Ibid.

It is important to note that the Rothschilds, whose holdings of Southern states securities were minimal and were only tangentially involved in the cotton trade, did not financially nor politically support the Confederacy. Rothschild records clearly reveal the firm's disdain for slavery. Nor, despite the myth, did the bank loan money to the Confederacy during the war.[43]

Sexton states in a footnote in regard to the 'myth' of Rothschild funding of the Confederacy that there is only one instance when the bank brokered (as distinct from purchased) a sale of Confederate bonds. This was for only $6,000, on behalf of Joseph Deynood in 1864. 'This sole instance pales in comparison to the hundreds of thousands of dollars worth of Union bonds that the bank brokered in the same period'.[44]

It was amidst this dire financial situation, denied the financial bloodline of international finance, that the Confederacy resorted to the issue of its equivalent to Lincoln's Greenbacks, the Graybacks, for which Davis is seldom acknowledged by those who present Lincoln as a champion of banking reform against usury.

---

43 Ibid., 151. Sexton's references to Rothschild disdain for slavery: 'N M Rothschild and Sons to [August] Belmont', 7 May, 9 July 1861, Rothschild Archive, London.

44 Ibid., 151; footnote 44.

Czar Nicholas Sacrificed
to the Golden Calf

Czarist Russia had a good reputation among Americans until an American journalist, George Kennan, was employed by international banker Jacob H Schiff of Kuhn Loeb and Company, Wall Street, to undertake both a smear campaign against Czarism as the greatest of tyrannies, and to sow revolutionary propaganda among Russian Prisoners of War in Japan during the 1904-1905 Russo-Japanese War.[1] While it could be argued that Schiff was primarily interested in helping his Jewish brethren by deposing the Czar, another major factor in the Czar's fate was the sovereignty of Russia's economy from international finance. As has been the case within the context of the West since the time of the Reformation, the 'revolts of the people' against supposed tyrannies, be they political or religious, have generally served the greater tyranny of Mammon.[2] Just as the Southern Confederacy has had bad PR that focuses on slavery, which has obscured its financial system, and the Axis states based around Germany, Japan and Italy have their economic achievements hidden by the academic focus upon war-time events, so Czarist Russia's bad PR has obscured the profound economic progress that was taking place without recourse to the usurers.

Anti-Czarist Agitation From USA

Robert Cowley states that during the Russo-Japanese War Kennan was in Japan organising Russian Prisoners Of War into "revolutionary cells" and Kennan claimed to have converted

---

1   K R Bolton, *Revolution from Above*, op. cit., 57-58.

2   Ibid., inter alia.

Csar Nicholas II - Last Emperor Of Russia

"52,000 Russian soldiers into 'revolutionists".[3] Cowley also adds, significantly, "Certainly such activity, well-financed by groups in the United States, contributed little to Russian-American solidarity."[4] Cowley quotes historian Thomas A Bailey as stating of Kennan in regard to undermining the former good relations between Russia and the USA: 'No one person did more to cause the people of the United States to turn against their presumed benefactor of yesteryear'.[5]

The source of the revolutionary funding 'by groups in the United States' was explained by Kennan at a celebration of the March 1917 Russian Revolution, reported by the *New York Times*:

Mr Kennan told of the work of the Friends of Russian Freedom in the revolution. He said that during the Russian-Japanese war he was in Tokyo, and that he was permitted to make visits among the 12,000 Russian prisoners in

---

3   Robert Cowley, 'A Year in Hell', *America and Russia: A Century and a Half of Dramatic Encounters*, ed. Oliver Jensen (New York: Simon and Schuster, 1962) 92-121.

4   Ibid., 120.

5   Ibid., 118.

Japanese hands at the end of the first year of the war. He had conceived the idea of putting revolutionary propaganda into the hands of the Russian army.

The Japanese authorities favoured it and gave him permission. After which he sent to America for all the Russian revolutionary literature to be had...

"The movement was financed by a New York banker you all know and love", he said, referring to Mr Schiff, " 'and soon we received a ton and a half of Russian revolutionary propaganda. At the end of the war 50,000 Russian officers and men went back to their country ardent revolutionists. The Friends of Russian Freedom had sowed 50,000 seeds of liberty in 100 Russian regiments. I do not know how many of these officers and men were in the Petrograd fortress last week, but we do know what part the army took in the revolution.'

Then was read a telegram from Jacob H Schiff, part of which is as follows: 'Will you say for me to those present at tonight's meeting how deeply I regret my inability to celebrate with the Friends of Russian Freedom the actual reward of what we had hoped and striven for these long years'.[6]

The reaction to the Russian revolution by Schiff and by other bankers in the USA and London, was one of jubilation. Schiff wrote enthusiastically to *The New York Times*:

May I through your columns give expression to my joy that the Russian nation, a great and good people, have at last effected their deliverance from centuries of autocratic oppression and through an almost bloodless revolution have now come into their own. Praised be God on high! Jacob H. Schiff.[7]

---

6   *New York Times*, 24 March 1917, 1-2.

7   Jacob H Schiff, 'Jacob H Schiff Rejoices, By Telegraph to the Editor of the New York

Writing to *The Evening Post* in response to a question about revolutionary Russia's new status with world financial markets, Schiff wrote:

> Replying to your request for my opinion of the effects of the revolution upon Russia's finances, I am quite convinced that with the certainty of the development of the country's enormous resources, which, with the shackles removed from a great people, will follow present events, Russia will before long take rank financially amongst the most favoured nations in the money markets of the world.[8]

Bankers Welcomed Czar's Overthrow

Schiff's reply reflected the general attitude of London and New York financial circles at the time of the revolution. John B Young of the National City Bank, who had been in Russia in 1916 in regard to a US loan, stated in 1917 of the revolution that it had been discussed widely when he had been in Russia the previous year. He regarded those involved as 'solid, responsible and conservative'.[9] In the same issue, *The New York Times* reported that there had been a rise in Russian exchange transactions in London 24 hours preceding the revolution, and that London had known of the revolution prior to New York. The article reported that most prominent financial and business leaders in London and New York had a positive view of the revolution.[10] Another report states that while there had been some disquiet about the revolution, 'this news was by no means unwelcome in more important banking circles'.[11]

Times', *New York Times*, 18 March, 1917. This can be viewed in The New York Times online archives: http://query.nytimes.com/mem/archive-free/pdf?res=9802E4DD163AE532A2575BC1A9659C946696D6CF

8   'Loans easier for Russia', *The New York Times*, 20 March 1917. http://query.nytimes.com/mem/archive-free/pdf?res=9B04EFDD143AE433A25753C2A9659C946696D6CF

9   'Is A People's Revolution', *The New York Times*, 16 March 1917.

10   'Bankers here pleased with news of revolution', ibid.

11   "Stocks strong – Wall Street interpretation of Russian News", ibid.

This is not the place to detail the fund of the Russian revolutionary movement and the subsequent relations between international finance and the Soviet Union after the Communist coup had deposed the rulers of the March 1917 Revolution. The reader is referred to this writer's book *Revolution from Above*.

Czarist Economic Policies

What we are concerned with here is why international bankers should welcome and even fund the Social Revolutionary party that overthrew the Czar in 1917. Here, as in the war against the Axis, the financial and economic system of Czarist Russia was not amenable to control by international finance.[12] Indeed, as far back as 1815 Nathan Mayer Rothschild approached Czar Alexander I at the Congress of Vienna and proposed setting up a central bank in Russia, that could be controlled like other central banks such as the Bank of England. The Czar declined. In 1860 the State Bank of the Russian Empire was established and until 1894 operated under the control of the Ministry of Finance. From 1894 it became the provider of credit to the commercial banks, through which low interest loans were provided to industry and commerce.[13]

Russia had the lowest National Debt of any world power, the lowest taxes, and the highest rates of economic growth in both agriculture and industry, with enviable labour laws. The picture is yet one of a tyranny founded on religious ignorance, abysmal working conditions, downtrodden serfs and multitudes of dissidents confined to appalling prisons.

Russia held more gold than any other power, and most significantly its state banknote issue was backed up 100% by these reserves.

---

12 George Knupffer, *The Struggle for World Power* (London: Plain Speaker Publishing Co., 1971), 138-146. Knupffer, was born during the reign of the last Czar, and become a leader of the Russian émigrés, serving as Chairman of the Russian Supreme Monarchist Council, and worked closely with Conservative Member of Parliament (1954-1971) and monetary reformer Captain Henry Kerby.

13 Stephen Goodson, '*The Truth About Imperial Russia*', http://rense.com/general95/truthaboutimpruss.html

Hence, credit and currency were not issued against a fraction of the gold on deposit but were fully backed by the reserves.[14] There was no need to borrow from private banks. In 1908 the National Debt stood at 58.7 roubles per inhabitant compared to 288 for France and 169.8 for Britain,[15] although Russia had just lost a war to Japan, while other powers had long been at peace. By 1914 83% of the interest and principal of the debt had been paid off by profits from the Russian State Railways.[16] The public debt in 1914 amounted to 8,825,000,000 roubles, most of which was contracted in Russia rather than from the foreign loan markets. In fact, before the war only 172,000,000 roubles had been loans from abroad.[17]

The Peasants' State Bank, founded in 1882, purchased land from wealthy proprietors and resold it to peasants by advancing long-term credit up to 90% of the value, at a low rate of interest, over an average period of 55 years. By 1914 80% of the arable land in European Russian was owned by peasants. Loans had gone from 222 million roubles in 1901 to 1,168 million in 1912.[18] In 1904 'People's Banks of Mutual Credit' were founded by the State, which extended rural credit operations. By 1914 there were 11,631,100 members.[19]

Among the most worrying aspects of Czarist Russia from the perspective of international finance was that Russia was 'autarchic' (economically self-sufficient), and she did not have a balance of trade deficit or a cumbersome debt to outside finance. Four-

---

14 George Knupffer, op. cit., 143.

15 Ibid., 144.

16 Ibid. 144.

17 Arsene de Goulevitch, *Czarism and Revolution* (Hawthorne, California: Omni Publications, 1962), 153. De Goulevitch served with the Air Force of the White Army fighting the Red Army during the Russian Civil War in 1918. During World War II he fought with the French Resistance in his adopted country, and in 1947 founded the Union for the Defence of Oppressed Peoples, opposing Communism. His comments are based on both Imperial and Soviet government statistics.

18 G Knupffer, *The Truth About the Reign of the Emperor Nicholas II* (London: Monarchist Press Association, ca. 1970), 11.

19 Arsene de Goulevitch, op. cit., 74.

fifths of the internal market was supplied by Russian industry.[20] Most capital investment for industry was derived from inside Russia. The financial market absorbed two-thirds of the total stocks and shares issued in Russia, i.e. 3,657,100,000 roubles, and only 1,509,300,000 roubles went abroad. Total foreign capital investment was 2,242,874,00 roubles, in comparison to the 19th century when most investment came from outside.[21] This autarchic industrial and rural development proceeded along with advanced social legislation which prompted US President Taft to state in 1912 to an audience of Russian dignitaries: 'Your Emperor has introduced legislation for the working classes more perfect than that which any of the democratic countries boast'. Prior to that, under Alexander III a factory inspectorate had already been established to oversee the working conditions in industry.[22]

It is not surprising, when the facts are garnered, that the international financial markets rejoiced at the fall of the Czar in March 1917. Czarist Russia up until 1917 was developing a self-sufficient home market that did not rely on either imports or outside loans, the two primary methods that international finance uses to control states. The situation changes when the 'dictatorship of the proletariat' was ostensibly established by the Bolsheviks who, until Stalin changed the direction of the USSR[23], sought to open Russia to foreign capital.

Ruskombank

In 1922 Soviet Russia's first international bank was created, Ruskombank, headed by Olof Aschberg of the Nye Banken, Stockholm, Sweden, who had advanced large sums to the Bolsheviks. The predominant capital represented in the bank was from 'The City'. The foreign director of Ruskombank was

---

20   Ibid., 94.

21   Ibid., 95.

22   Ibid., 96.

23   K R Bolton, *Stalin: The Enduring Legacy* (London: Black House Publishing, 2012).

Max May, vice president of the Guaranty Trust Company, Wall Street, a J P Morgan interest.[24]

Guaranty Trust Company became intimately involved with Soviet economic transactions. A *Scotland Yard Intelligence Report* stated as early as 1919 the connection between Guaranty Trust and Ludwig C A K Martens, head of the Soviet Bureau in New York when the bureau was established that year.[25]

When representatives of the Lusk Committee investigating Bolshevik activities in the USA raided the Soviet Bureau offices on 7 May 1919, files of communications with almost a thousand US firms were found. Basil H Thompson of Scotland Yard in the special report stated that despite denials, there was evidence in the seized files that the Soviet Bureau was being funded by Guaranty Trust Company.[26] It was also J P Morgan interests that predominated in the formation of a consortium, the American International Corporation (AIC), which was another source eager to secure the recognition of the still embryonic Soviet state. Interests represented in the directorship of the American International Corporation included the National City Bank; General Electric; Du Pont; Kuhn, Loeb and Co.; Federal Reserve Bank of New York; Ingersoll-Rand; Hanover National Bank, Rockefeller interests and others.[27]

24   Antony Sutton, *Wall Street and the Bolshevik Revolution* (New York: Arlington House Publishers, 1974), 62-63.

25   'Scotland Yard Intelligence Report', London 1919, US State Dept. Decimal File, 316-22-656, cited by Sutton ibid., 113.

26   Basil H Thompson, British Home Office Directorate of Intelligence, 'Special Report No. 5 (Secret)', Scotland Yard, London, July 14, 1919; cited by Sutton, ibid., 115.

27   Sutton, op.cit. 130-131.

The Real Right's Answer To
Socialism & Capitalism

'Modern capitalism is just as subversive as Marxism'.
Julius Evola

It can be noted here that in contrast to the relationship between the early Soviet State and international capital, and the fact that the USSR never did succeed in freeing herself from borrowing from international finance, one of the leading apologists for Czarism in exile, George Knupffer, recognised the importance of state credit as an integral policy for any genuinely 'Right-wing' party. This contrasts with parties that are called 'Right-wing' but are really Whig-Liberals (i.e. Free Trade). Knupffer realised that Socialism can only be defeated by treating the root cause of social injustice: debt-finance. Knupffer wrote of what should be the outlook of genuine Rightists:

A sustained attack must be begun upon the economic, political and social teachings and practises of the enemy in their Capitalistic and Socialistic forms. It is useless to attack materialism in theory, but leave real power in the hands of its adepts. ... We are by no means afraid of using the word Right... While we have stated that the Right is Christian, we have also said that men of other Faiths can also be of the Right. We would feel certain that all of those who put the spirit about things material, duty above greed and love above hate and envy are in the camp, of the Organic Right. ... In practical as well as philosophical terms there is no fight between the Capitalist system, based on usury, and communism, since the former created the latter and gives it every support while pretending to oppose it; both are concerned with the identical aim of founding the materialistic world state.[1]

Rightist Programme Against Usury

Knupffer summarises one of the main premises of his book, vis-à-vis the Right and the role of international finance and usury:

> By usurping the power to issue the means of exchange in all forms, once the sovereign right and duty of the heads of states, the money-lenders have succeeded in establishing their rule over every nation in the world. But that rule is unstable, as the ever-growing debt stricture and the need to collect interest on all money in circulation puts an intolerable strain on all forms of enterprise, so that it must eventually lead to a collapse of the system, or to war. Therefore the financiers themselves create Communism as a future substitute whereby to perpetuate their rule through terrorism. Meanwhile Capitalism must sustain its structure by the imposition of an ever-growing burden of taxation.[2]

Four decades later, and in the midst of the global debt crisis, rioting and US wars against states reticent about the much touted 'new world order', Knupffer's words seem prophetic. However, anyone with an understanding of the processes and power of debt-finance would have easily made such predictions. Of the twelve planks as the basis for a 'Party of the Right' monetary reform takes a major place:

1. That one of the basic duties of the State, the issue of money in all forms free of debt or interest and in the right amounts should revert to the Crown [or President].

---

1   George Knupffer, op. cit., 205-207.

2   Ibid., 207.

2. That the National Debt should be gradually abolished and all private debts be made subject to amortization.

3. That as a consequence of the foregoing there should be no longer any Income Tax and only such indirect taxes as are absolutely necessary to cover the proper expenses of the Government.

4. That, in view of the great increase in prosperity which will result from the proposed financial and economic reforms, and in view of the consequences of increasing automation, there should be a gradual reduction in the hours per week worked by most employees making allowance, however, for the effects of new enterprises and diversification of production and services.

5. That the indirect ownership of business through instruments of perpetual indebtedness should, gradually be replaced by direct ownership with full responsibility by individuals, partnerships or co-operatives.

6. That the representation and influence of individuals and groups in the political and social life of the realm should be governed by their value to the community and their experiences and knowledge, expressed directly and not through parties controlled by financiers.[3]

Beyond The Economic Treadmill

Point 4 of Knupffer's programme now seems strange, given that working hours have increased, rather than decreased, despite the leaps and bounds of automation. The drudgery of the new 'IT' economy has not only not lessened working hours, but have concomitantly also increased by leaps and bounds, accompanied moreover by the steady lengthening of the working age until

---

3   Ibid., 'Aims and Principles of a Proposed Party of the Right', 210-211.

retirement, until a few years remain of one's life beyond work. A 'Mercer global research report' on raising the retirement age examined forty-seven countries, showing that many 'developed' countries intend raising the retirement age, with the UK at a maximum of 68 years.[4] Citing Australian statistics Hamilton and Dennis state that, 'only 28 percent of employees work a standard week of between 35 and 40 hours', with a high of 15 percent working more than 60 hours. 'The proportion of men working these hours has grown substantially in the past twenty years,' but the trend is also increasing among women.[5] The conclusion is that: 'The research indicates that a significant proportion of the total workforce are working 50 hours or more per week....'[6] The importance of leisure in the building of culture was central to Medieval life. The work ethic of those times, as distinct from the Puritan work ethic that still dominates the West, albeit in secularised form, is explained below.

The reduction of working hours was – and is - a primary aim of Social Credit. However working hours are ever longer, regardless of automation, again largely due to the debt factor, including the necessity of two income families to pay mortgages and other debts, and the added recent factor of spiralling credit card debt.

One of the premises of the 'new economics', or Social Credit, is that the machine is a cultural legacy, an inheritance that belongs to humanity in general, or to be more precise, largely to Western man. It is the product of accumulated work and thought, and any benefits accruing therefrom should be given as a 'National Dividend' of that cultural legacy to all.

---

4   Mercer Wealth Solutions (2011), Mercer Global Report, 'Governments Increase Retirement Ages to Curb Rising Costs', https://www.mercersupertrust.co.nz/latest-news.asp?articleId=1061

5   C Hamilton and R Denniss, *Affluenza: When too Much is Never Enough*, (New South Wales: Allen and Unwin, 2005), 86.

6   L Fursman, (2008), Working Long Hours in New Zealand: A Profile of Long Hours Workers Using Data from the 2006 Census, Department of Labour, Wellington, http://dol.govt.nz/publication-view.asp?ID=256

The ethics behind this was described by one of its proponents, writing that, '...the Machine is no sudden miracle descended on man out of the blue, but that it is on the contrary an inheritance, definite, logical and ours. It is not a gift... it is the result of effort, man's effort, and the result of work, man's work'; the 'corporate wealth inherent in the Machine' is the legacy of all'. Therefore, full employment is not an economic question but an ethical question. Full employment is not a panacea. What is an economic necessity is the sufficiency of purchasing power to consume production, regardless of the amount of time and years expended on work. Once this is understood, the 'dole', so derided by many, is what the 'new economics' referred to as a 'social dividend'.[7]

C H Douglas' 'social credit' theory questioned whether 'full employment' should be the primary concern of economics, contending that the 'dole', despite its 'stigma' as 'charity' is nothing but 'a claim on goods ... of which the persons from whom it is collected in taxation already have enough for their needs...'; and that the wage is not the only means for which to distribute purchasing power. Douglas held that there is no justification 'for suggesting that even a large number of commercially unemployed necessarily threatens the material welfare of the community...'[8] As for leisure, including the 'forced leisure of unemployment', Douglas rejected the belief, as common today as then, that it is in some manner 'detrimental'. What is detrimental is idleness that is not utilised to embark on higher pursuits in life, whether it is learning a musical instrument, reading a book or spending more time with one's children. That is a social, cultural and spiritual problem, not one of economics. Although anathema to most Social Crediters, it was a problem that National Socialist Germany, Fascist Italy by the organisation of the 'Strength Through Joy' and 'Afterwork' programmes respectively,[9] where working families could enjoy symphony orchestras, or

---

7   M Colbourne, (1934), *Economic Nationalism*, Figurehead, London, 72-73.

8   C H Douglas, (1937), *Social Credit*, Eyre and Spottiswood, London, 114.

9   G Berghaus, *Fascism and Theatre* (Oxford: Berghahn Books, 1996).

holiday on cruise liners at nominal prices. The intention of such programmes was to elevate the masses of people, not to push everyone down to a dead level of 'proletarian' equality. After so many generations of Capitalist drudgery and cultural deadening, it would be necessary for the State – ideally through the trades and professional associations and unions, functioning as Guilds - to take the lead in providing options for the fulfilment of one's life towards higher ends in a more leisured society.

What Knupffer explained has now been largely forgotten and he was among the last of a generation who understood the true meaning of the Right, and of Conservatism, which are not at all intended to be a defence of the conservation of Capitalism.

Common Outlook Of Marxism & Capitalism

Oswald Spengler, one of the seminal philosopher-historians of the 'revolutionary Conservative movement,[10] explained what Knupffer had also sought to show, the common outlook between Capitalism and Communism. He sought to redefine 'Socialism' as an ethical system based on the duty of all classes towards the commonweal, as distinct from Marxism and similar Leftist movements that are merely variations of Capitalism:

> Socialism contains elements that are older, stronger, and more fundamental than his [Marx's] critique of society. Such elements existed without him and continued to develop without him, in fact contrary to him. They are not to be found on paper; they are in the blood. And only the blood can decide the future.[11]

Spengler in his magnum opus, *The Decline of The West*, stated that in the late epoch of a Civilization, in which The West has

---

10   See: T Southgate (ed.) *Spengler: Thoughts & Perspectives Volume 11* (London: Black Front Press, 2012).

11   Oswald Spengler (1919) *Prussiaism and Socialism*, online at: http://archive.org/details/PrussianismAndSocialism

been for several centuries, there is a reaction against the rule of money, which restores tradition:

> If we call these money-powers 'Capitalism', then we may designate as Socialism the will to call into life a mighty politico-economic order that transcends all class interests, a system of lofty thoughtfulness and duty-sense that keeps the whole in fine condition for the decisive battle of its history, and this battle is also the battle of money and law. The private powers of the economy want free paths for their acquisition of great resources...[12]

In a footnote to the above Spengler reminded readers regarding 'Capitalism' that, 'in this sense the interest-politics of the workers' movements also belong to it, in that their object is not to overcome money-values, but to possess them'. As seen above, Knupffer, and the Right in general, realised the identity between Capitalism and the Left and the 'hidden hand' of international finance behind them both.[13] Knupffer described the Rightist sense of duty in similar terms to Spengler's ethical 'Socialism', like Spengler contrasting it with the capitalistic outlook of the Left:

> ... Be it the usury-capitalism of the golden International, or the communism of the Red international, the ultimate aim of all false democracy, liberalism and 'progress', all lead to universal power and almost limitless profits for the intended bosses, who are behind the scenes and are not the leaders of the intermediary phases of the Revolution.

Therefore phraseology apart, at the roots, the revolutionary, whatever his nominal label, from mild bourgeois liberal to murdering communist, is, consciously or not, fighting for profit. Intellectually, emotionally and instinctively, he is urged on by materialism, even if he still practises some religion. Thus it is inevitable that the end product of the

---

12   Spengler *The Decline of The West*, op. cit., Vol. 2, 506.

13   Cf. K R Bolton, *Revolution from Above*, op. cit.

Revolution must be slavery and misery, except for the intended final beneficiaries, as yet half-hidden operators of the game.

On the other hand, the true Counter-Revolutionary, even if not devoid of some self-interests or ambition, is in all respects a genuine fighter for the best interests of all the people everywhere. His sense of duty and sacrifice will always be dominant over any other considerations.[14]

Hence, Marxism and all other forms of Left-socialism based on economics, is a reflection of capitalism, not a revolt against it. The original 'Tories', the Cavaliers fighting against Cromwell's Puritans, were the precursors of the 'Right' in the English-speaking world, as the English Conservative philosopher Anthony Ludovici pointed out. In France where the terms 'Right' and 'Left' originate, it was the Republicans and the most extreme party, the Jacobins, who were the precursors of both Marxism-communism and the Whig-Liberalism of the newly emerging merchant class.

Spengler called the Left 'capitalistic' because it does not aim to replace money-based values, 'but to possess them'. He stated of Marxism that it is 'nothing but a trusty henchman of Big Capital, which knows perfectly well how to make use of it'.[15] It is a phenomenon that has arisen in the same cycles of previous Civilisations, Spengler referring to the Roman in comparison to our own times:

> The concepts of Liberalism and Socialism are set in effective motion only by money. It was the *Equites*, the big-money party, which made Tiberius Gracchu's popular movement possible at all; and as soon as that part of the reforms that was advantageous to themselves had been successfully legalized, they withdrew and the movement collapsed. There is no proletarian, not even a communist, movement

---

14   George Knupffer, op. cit., 209.

15   Spengler, *The Decline of The West*, op. cit., Vol. 2, p. 464.

that has not operated in the interests of money, in the directions indicated by money, and for the time permitted by money — and that without the idealist amongst its leaders having the slightest suspicion of the fact.[16]

The Italian Revolutionary Conservative historian-philosopher, Julius Evola, likewise observed that 'the antithesis between capitalism and Marxism' is a 'pseudo-antithesis'; a false opposition. Having the hindsight of seeing how Marxist and Capitalist societies were working out a century after Marx wrote *The Communist Manifesto*, Evola observed that,

...In free-market economies, as well as in Marxist societies, the myth of production and its corollaries (e.g. standardisation, monopolies, cartels, technocracy) are subject to the "hegemony" of the economy, becoming the primary factor on which the material conditions of existence are based. Both systems regard as 'backward' or as 'underdeveloped' those civilisations that do not amount to 'civilisations based on labour and production' – namely, those civilisations that, luckily for themselves, have not yet caught up in the feverish industrial exploitation of every natural resource, the social and productive enslavement of all human possibilities, and the exaltation of technical and industrial standards; in other words, those civilisations that still enjoy a certain space and relative freedom.[17]

Today we are witnessing the mopping up of those few remaining traditional societies that still existed in Evola's time, that could not be bought off by world trade and loans, the most recent as this is written being the 'Arab Spring', and the actions against Iran and Syria, contrived – again in the name of 'the people' – by plutocrats such as George Soros, and the world-reformers of the

---

16   Ibid. p. 402.

17   J Evola, *Men Among the Ruins* (Rochester, Vermont: Inner Traditions International, 2002), 167-168.

US State Department, National Endowment for Democracy, and a vast array of other think tanks, and NGO's, who plan and fund the so-called 'colour revolutions'.[18]

Capitalism in Marxist Dialectics

While what is popularly described today as 'Right-wing' is claimed as the custodian of 'free trade' and the advocate of the free play of 'market forces', whereby any intervention by the State is regarded with outrage, Karl Marx understood the subversive, anti-Conservative character of Free Trade. Spengler cites Marx as stating of Free Trade in 1847:

> Generally speaking, the protectionist system today is conservative, whereas the Free Trade system has a destructive effect. It destroys the former nationalities and renders the contrast between proletariat and bourgeois more acute. In a word, the Free Trade system is precipitating the social revolution. And only in this revolutionary sense do I vote for Free Trade.[19]

For Marx capitalism was part of an inexorable process of history, called dialectical materialism that sees humanity ascending from Primitive Communism, through Feudalism, Capitalism, Socialism and ultimately – as the end of history – to the millennial utopia of Communism. Throughout this dialectical unfolding the motive force of history is class struggle with the servant class fighting the ruling class for supremacy, based on economic relations. In the Marxist theory of history everything is reduced to the struggle of,

> freeman and slave, patrician and plebeian, lord and serf, guild master and journeyman, in a word, oppressor and oppressed... in constant opposition to one another, carried

---

18   CF. K R Bolton, *Revolution from Above*, op. cit., especially 213-244.

19   Spengler, *The Hour of Decision*, op. cit., 141; citing Marx, Appendix to Elend der Philosophie, 1847.

on uninterrupted, now hidden, now open, a fight that each time ended, either in a revolutionary re-constitution of society at large, or in the common ruin of the contending classes.[20]

From a Rightist view, Marx correctly described the role of Capitalism in the destruction of traditional society and went on to describe what we today call 'globalization'. Those who advocate Free Trade while calling themselves Conservatives might like to consider why Marx supported Free Trade and described it as both 'destructive' and as 'revolutionary'. Marx saw it as the necessary stage of the dialectic process that is imposing universal standardisation.

Marx in describing the dialectical role of Capitalism, stated that wherever the 'bourgeoisie' or merchant 'has got the upper hand [he] has put an end to all feudal, patriarchal, idyllic relations'. The bourgeoisie (who in traditional societies have a subordinated rather than a controlling role) 'has pitilessly torn asunder' feudal bonds, and 'has left remaining no other nexus between man and man than naked self-interest', and 'callous cash payment'. It has, among other things, 'drowned' religiosity and chivalry 'in the icy water of egotistical calculation'. 'It has resolved personal worth into exchange value, and in place of the numberless indefeasible chartered freedoms, has set up that single, unconscionable freedom – Free Trade'.[21]

What Knupffer called the 'Organic Right' would agree with Marx's assessment on the destructive effects of Capitalism. Where the 'Organic Right' stands in opposition to Marx is in his regarding the process as both inevitable and desirable.

Marx condemned opposition to this dialectical process as 'reactionary'. Indeed it is, or what many such as Knupffer

---

20   K Marx, *The Communist Manifesto* (Moscow: Progress Publishers, 1975), 41.

21   Ibid., 44.

called 'Counter-Revolutionary'.[22] The 'Organic Right' is both 'revolutionary' and 'Conservative in-so-far as it advocates the literal meaning of a 'revolution', the return of a cycle, with an axis in the centre; the axis being man's connexion with the Divine, whether one wants to accept it in a literal or in a symbolic sense. Marx was here defending Communists against claims by "Reactionaries" that his system would result in the destruction of the traditional family, and relegate the professions to mere 'wage-labour' by stating that this was already being done by capitalism anyway and is therefore not a process that is to be resisted – which is 'Reactionism' – but welcomed as a necessary stage towards Communism.

Uniformity of Production & Culture

Marx saw the constant need for the revolutionising of the instruments of production as inevitable under capitalism. This in turn brought society into a continual state of flux, of 'everlasting uncertainty and agitation', which distinguishes the 'bourgeoisie epoch from all other ones'.[23] The 'need for a constantly expanding market' means that capitalism spreads globally, and thereby gives a 'cosmopolitan character' to 'modes of production and consumption in every country'. This in Marxist dialectics is a necessary part of destroying national boundaries and distinctive cultures as a prelude to world Communism. It is capitalism that establishes the basis for internationalism. Therefore, when the Leftist rants against globalisation he does so as rhetoric in the pursuit of a political agenda; not from ethical opposition to globalisation.

Marx identified the opponents of this globalisation process not as Leftists but, on the contrary, as 'Reactionists'. The reactionaries are appalled that the old local and national industries are being destroyed, self-sufficiency is being undermined, and 'we have… universal inter-dependence of nations', Marx wrote. Likewise

---

22   George Knupffer, op. cit., 208.

23   K Marx,op. cit., 47.

in the cultural sphere, where 'national and local literatures' are displaced by 'a world literature'.[24]

With this standardisation of the means of production comes a loss of meaning of being part of a craft or a profession. Obsession with work becomes as an end in itself, which fails to provide higher meaning because of its being reduced to that of a solely economic function. Marx said of this in relation to the ruin of the traditional order:

> Owing to the extensive use of machinery and to division of labour, the work of the proletarians has lost all individual character, and, consequently, all charm for the workman. He becomes an appendage of the machine, and it is only the most simple, most monotonous, and the most easily acquired knack, that is required of him...[25]

Whereas the Medieval guilds fulfilled a role that was religious and cultural, these have been replaced by the trades unions as nothing more than instruments of economic competition. The entirety of civilization has become an expression of money-values, but preoccupation of the Gross Domestic Product cannot be a substitute for more profound human meaning.

Reactionism

Marx points out in *The Communist Manifesto* that 'Reactionists' (sic) view with 'great chagrin'[26] this dialectical processes of Capitalism. The Reactionary, or the 'Rightist', is the anti-Capitalist *par excellence*, because he is above and beyond the outlook from which both Capitalism and Marxism emerged in 19th Century England, and he rejects *in total* this economic outlook on which both are founded. As Knupffer, Spengler and others pointed out, both are materialistic. Thus the word

---

24 Ibid., pp. 46-47.

25 Ibid., 51.

26 Ibid, 46.

'Reactionary', usually used in a derogatory sense, can be accepted as an accurate term for what is required for a 'Counter-Revolution against Capitalism, and its twin Marxism.

Marx condemned resistance to the dialectical process of Capitalism as 'Reactionist':

> The lower middle class, the small manufacturer, the shopkeeper, the artisan, the peasant. All these fight against the bourgeoisie, to save from extinction their existence as fractions of the middle class. They are therefore not revolutionary, but conservative. Nay more, they are reactionary, for they try to roll back the wheel of history. If by chance they are revolutionary, they are so only in view of their impending transfer into the proletariat, they thus defend not their present, but their future interests, they desert their own standpoint to place themselves at that of the proletariat.[27]

This so-called 'lower middle class' is therefore inexorably condemned to the purgatory of proletarian dispossession until such time as it recognises its historical revolutionary class role. This 'lower middle class' can either emerge from this class purgatory by joining the ranks of the proletarian chosen people, become part of the Leftist revolution and enter a new millennium, or it can descend from its class purgatory, if it insists on trying to maintain the traditional order, and be consigned to oblivion, which might be hastened by the firing squads of Bolshevism.

Marx devoted section three of his *Communist Manifesto* to a repudiation of 'reactionary socialism'. He condemned the 'feudal socialism' that arose among the remnants of the aristocracy that sought to join forces with the 'working class' against the new mercantile society of machines and mills. Marx stated that the aristocracy, in trying to reassert their pre-bourgeoisie position, had actually lost sight of their own class interests in having

---

27   Ibid., 57.

to side with the proletariat.[28] This is nonsense. An alliance of the dispossessed artisans and peasants into what had become the so-called 'proletariat', with the increasingly dispossessed aristocracy, is an organic alliance, which finds its enemies as much in Marxism as in Capitalism.

Marx raged against this budding alliance between the aristocracy and the dispossessed crafts. Hence, Marx condemned 'feudal socialism' as 'half echo of the past, half menace of the future'.[29] Again, Marx was on to something, but only in his rejection of it: the 'Organic Right' and the 'Counter-Revolution', the ethical-Socialism described by Spengler, which equates with the 'Reactionary Socialism' condemned by Marx, looks Janus-like to the past and to the future. Its Counter-Revolution is based on tradition, while that of Marx is based on the destruction of tradition.

This 'Reactionism' was a movement that enjoyed significant support among craftsmen, clergymen, nobles and literati in Germany in 1848, the year *The Communist Manifesto* was published. This movement repudiated the Free Market that had divorced the individual from Church, State and community, 'and placed egoism and self-interest before subordination, commonality, and social solidarity'.[30] Max Beer, an historian of German Socialism, stated of these 'Reactionists':

The modern era seemed to them to be built on quicksands, to be chaos, anarchy, or an utterly unmoral and godless outburst of intellectual and economic forces, which must inevitably lead to acute social antagonism, to extremes of wealth and poverty, and to a universal upheaval. In this frame of mind, the Middle Ages, with its firm order in

---

28   Ibid., III 'Socialist and Communist Literature, 1. Reactionary Socialism, a. Feudal Socialism', 77.

29   Ibid., p. 78.

30   M Beer, *A General History of Socialism and Social Struggle*, (New York: Russell and Russell, 1957) Vol. 2, 109.

Church, economic and social life, its faith in God, its feudal tenures, its cloisters, its autonomous associations and its guilds appeared to these thinkers like a well-compacted building...[31]

It is just such an alliance of all classes that is required to resist the common subversive phenomena of Capitalism and the Left. If the Right wishes to restore the health of the cultural organism that is based on traditional values, then it cannot do so by embracing economic doctrines that are themselves subversive, and were welcomed by Marx as part of a subversive process.

What Marx condemned as 'Reactionism' Julius Evola called 'a true restorative reaction'. Evola suggests that a new social order can be achieved by looking at the craftsmen's 'Corporations' of Classical Rome and the Guilds of the Romano-Germanic Middle Ages. The West's Middle Ages have been distorted with references to lack of democracy and equality, and other banal concepts very meaningful to the present age. However, Juliet Schor, Professor of Economics at Harvard University, has shown that Medieval Europe accorded much more leisure and freedom than the present system of Free Trade:

> One of capitalism's most durable myths is that it has reduced human toil. This myth is typically defended by a comparison of the modern forty-hour week with its seventy- or eighty-hour counterpart in the nineteenth century. The implicit - but rarely articulated - assumption is that the eighty-hour standard has prevailed for centuries....

> ...Before capitalism, most people did not work very long hours at all. The tempo of life was slow, even leisurely; the pace of work relaxed. Our ancestors may not have been rich, but they had an abundance of leisure. When capitalism raised their incomes, it also took away their time...

---

31   Ibid., 88-89.

All told, holiday leisure time in medieval England took up probably about one-third of the year. And the English were apparently working harder than their neighbors....[32]

This description by Professor Schor of the work ethos of the Medieval epoch illustrates Evola's statement that work has now become an end in itself, which would have been regarded as insane at that time. There is now a veritable cult of work, despite the increasing numbers of unemployed and other beneficiaries, who are widely denigrated by those who do work. The ethos is that of the Puritan, whose work ethic precluded higher cultural pursuits. It is a secularised Puritanism. Hence the unemployed artist for example, who is drawing a benefit, will be regarded with derision by society at large; not on the basis of whether his art is of cultural merit, but solely because he is not part of the mass production process. Evola states of traditional societies in this regard:

No economic value was cherished enough to sacrifice one's independence to it, nor was the quest for the means of subsistence deemed worthy to consume one's entire life. Overall, the above-mentioned truth was acknowledged – that human progress must be defined not on an economic and social level, but rather on an inner plane; in other words, progress does not consist in leaving behind one's ranks 'to become successful', or in increasing the amount of work in order to gain a position that one is not qualified for...[33]

Max Weber in discussing the Puritan ethic of Capitalism writes that it was contrary to that of the Medieval view, stating that for Thomas Aquinas[34]

---

32 Juliet B Schor, *The Overworked American: The Unexpected Decline of Leisure*, 'Introduction', (New York: Basic Books, 1992), http://groups.csail.mit.edu/mac/users/rauch/worktime/hours_workweek.html

33 J Evola, *Men Among the Ruins*, op. cit., 172.

34 Thomas Aquinas (1225-1274) seminal philosopher and Doctor of the Church. See: Ralph McInerny and John O'Callaghan, 'Saint Thomas Aquinas', *The Stanford*

...labour is only necessary *naturali ratione* for the maintenance of individual and community. Where this end is achieved, the precept ceases to have any meaning. Moreover, it holds only for the race, not for every individual. It does not apply to anyone who can live without 'labour on his possessions', and of course contemplation, as a spiritual form of action...[35]

The Reformation was a prelude to other Revolutions against the traditional order. Its effects remain with us, and are indeed pervasive regardless of the decline of religious faith. The Reformation gave a moral justification for Capitalism, which continues to be the moral foundation of Western societies. Weber explained the difference between the outlooks of Medieval and Capitalist societies:

The real moral objection is to relaxation in the security of possession, the enjoyment of wealth with the consequence of idleness and the temptations of the flesh, above all of distraction from the pursuit of a righteous life. In fact, it is only because possession involves this danger of relaxation that it is objectionable at all. For the saints' everlasting rest is in the next world; on earth man must, to be certain of his state of grace, 'do the works of him who sent him, as long as it is yet day'. Here the difference from the medieval view-point becomes quite evident. [36]

Weber continues that artistic pursuits were anathema to the utilitarian outlook of the Puritans, writing of the new order that Cromwell brought to England:

The theatre was obnoxious to the Puritans, and with the

Encyclopedia of Philosophy (Winter 2010 Edition), Edward N Zalta (ed.), http://plato.stanford.edu/archives/win2010/entries/aquinas/

35   M Weber, *The Protestant Ethic and the Spirit of Capitalism*, Asceticism and the Sprit of Capitalism (London: Unwin Hyman, 1930), Chapter 5. .

36   Ibid.

strict exclusion of the erotic and of nudity from the realm of toleration, a radical view of either literature or art could not exist. The conceptions of idle talk, of superfluities, and of vain ostentation, all designations of an irrational attitude without objective purpose, thus not ascetic, and especially not serving the glory of God, but of man, were always at hand to serve in deciding in favour of sober utility as against any artistic tendencies.[37]

Evola pointed to the obsession with 'work' and making the means the end, as not sane. Those who reject belief in what Evola called the modern West's 'sacred cow' of labour are regarded as freeloaders. Evola deplored tendencies of what is referred to as the 'economic treadmill'. Admittedly, this treadmill is now more than ever difficult for the individual to get off, because debt – the very issue we have been discussing - enslaves everyone, great and small, from individuals, to families to entire nations. The Capitalist answer to an economic system that now seems to have gotten out of control is to extend the retirement age, so that the payment of benefits can be delayed, and perhaps large numbers of individuals will die off while working before they retire. A 'Mercer global research report' on raising the retirement age examined forty-seven countries, showing that many 'developed' countries intend raising the retirement age, with the United Kingdom aiming for a maximum of 68 years.[38] Working hours are also being constantly extended and the forty-hour week has evaporated. It seems that now there is no escape from the economic treadmill other than through death. The Medieval peasant and artisan would have looked upon our Free Market society with dread.

Some economists are questioning what Evola considered a 'perverse' attitude towards work, in what has been called

---

37   Ibid.

38   Mercer Wealth Solutions (2011), Mercer Global Report, 'Governments Increase Retirement Ages to Curb Rising Costs', https://www.mercersupertrust.co.nz/latest-news.asp?articleId=1061

affluenza, the pursuit of affluence as a pathological symptom, which accords well with Evola's attitude to the same phenomenon. Two contemporary economists have written:

> Despite the barrage of advertising that tries to tell us otherwise, the more materialistic we are the less free we are. Why? Because we must commit more of our lives to working to pay for our material desires. And the more acquisitive we are the more desires and the means of satisfying them are determined by others. Acquisitive people derive their identity and their imagined place in society from the things they own, yet the symbols, that confer self-worth and status are at the whim of external forces... Materialism thus robs us of autonomy.[39]

Evola drew a distinction between the cult of *work* as a perverse notion, and the concept of *action* motivated by forces higher than the material. This work cult is the proletarian view of life encouraged by Capitalism, and idolised by Marx. The Rightist 'task ahead' is to 'deproletarianise the view of life'.[40] We can see the 'proletarian view' today among all sectors of society that esteem 'work' as the highest of earthly pursuits, and especially among the capitalistic classes. It is a type of secularised Puritanism that sees leisure as ungodly and the pursuit of artistic goals that leisure allows, as frivolous.[41]

Evola refers to a Buddhist text about a man who is running under the intense sun, who eventually stops to ask 'why?' What results from this questioning of the means having become the end is 'inner transformation or *metanoia*', in order to gain 'inner freedom', not for the purpose of establishing a 'renunciatory, utopian and miserable civilisation', but of restoring a 'real hierarchy of values'. This liberation applies not only to the individual but to the whole

---

39   C Hamilton and R Denniss, (2005), *Affluenza: When too much is Never Enough*, (New South Wales: Allen and Unwin), 15.

40   J Evola, *Men Among the Ruins*, op. cit., 175.

41   M Weber, op. cit.

of society, including the State when it relies on outside economic forces – international finance capital - that limit the possibilities of the State. Evola insisted that if a standard of material living must be sacrificed for the sake of freedom, and for becoming aloof from world economic control, then *autarchy* or national economic self-sufficiency becomes an ethical imperative; and *austerity* is better than servitude to plutocrats. A remnant of the traditional ideas still exists in some societies, such as in India and in some Islamic states, where the spiritual life for the masses of people of all classes takes precedence over the accumulation of material possession, but these and the states, cultures and peoples that Western plutocrats and commentators call 'underdeveloped', upon which they seek to impose – by force, if necessary – a universal standard based on production and consumption. As Traditionalists know, it is the modern West that is impoverished, spiritually, leading to suicide, alienation, a sense of purposeless, selfishness, family and marital breakdown, rampant abortion, alcoholism, crime and drug addiction…

Homo Oeconomicus

In a traditional society economics is subservient. In the 'modern' era of a Civilisation economics rules. The result is the aberration called *homo oeconomicus*: Economic Man. It is a new species formed by economic forces, who is detached from faith, land, community, culture, duty, sacrifice, and any notion of the eternal character of family. Evola writes that economics has a 'body and soul of its own, and inner moral factors have always determined its meaning and spirit'.[42]

> Such spirit… should be distinguished from the various forms of production, distribution and organisation of economic goods; it may vary depending on individual instances and it bestows a very different scope and meaning on the economic factor.[43]

---

42   J Evola, op. cit., 168.

43   Ibid., 168.

It was this economic 'body and soul' upon which the Medieval Guilds were based. The economics of Marxism and Capitalism have no 'body and soul'. Evola wrote that,

> the pure *homo oeconomicus* is a fiction or the by-product of an evidentially degenerated specialisation. This, in every normal civilisation, a purely economic man – that is, the one who sees the economy not as an order of means but rather as an order of ends to which he dedicates his main activities – was always rightly regarded as a man of lower social extraction: lower in a spiritual sense, and furthermore in a social or political one.[44]

In contrast to 'modern' humanity the citizen of the Medieval community prior to the Reformation viewed himself as part of a co-operative social organism. The American economist W D P Bliss, writing of Nuremberg, but also pointing out that the situation applied all over 'Germanic Europe' until the Reformation, described a society where 'the master worked beside the artisan'.[45]

> Every Nuremberger, like every Medieval man, thought of himself, not as an independent unit, but as a dependent, although component, part of a larger organism, church or empire or city or guild. This was the very essence of medieval life... [46]

This was the 'Reactionism' scathingly condemned by Marx. In this 'Reactionism' Marx saw the means by which his so-called 'inexorable wheel of history' could be turned towards another direction that returned the human to a place beyond the most animalistic and debased levels of existence upheld alike by Capitalism and its Left-wing offspring.

---

44 Ibid.

45 W D P Bliss, *New Encyclopaedia of Social Reform*, (New York: Funk and Wagnalls, 1908), 545.

46 Ibid., 546.

Conclusion

Breaking the bondage of usury can be done and has been done. Indeed, the natural state of human society is not one of debt but one of the creative – as distinct from the parasitic – exchange of goods and services. In primeval times and later, this exchange was done by barter, and involved merely exchanging one's produce for what was made or grown by one's neighbour, often at a village market. Credit and currency were introduced as a convenient means for the same purpose: the exchange of goods and services; a mere token. In later centuries credit and currency became commodities in themselves, instead of just tokens, and profit was made in the form of interest (usury). Money-lenders persuaded Kings that they could deal with finance better than the Throne, and as if by magic they could make money out of nothing so long as they got paid back in real money based on real work, plus a profit (interest).

That is how 'modern' banking' works. That is how we get in return booms and busts, recessions and depressions, credit squeezes, inflation and deflation, deficits, mortgages, and pervasive debt, from an individual's credit card to entire nations. It is how money-lenders, condemned by both the Catholic Church and Islam, driven from the Temple by Jesus, control the fate of individuals, families, businesses, communities, nations, and the entire world. What was condemned by Islam and Catholics as 'sin' and prohibited is now regarded as a respectable business.

The answer to the money-lenders is to throw them out, as Jesus made a scourge and threw them out of the Temple. Any nation that embarks on that course however, requires the stamina to resist a power that has at its disposal not only the means of imposing trade embargoes, but the wherewithal to bomb a nation into submission. However, as a parasite destroys its host and ultimately must flee to another host or die with that host, so the parasitic money system will implode. The question that remains is that in the aftermath, will a new system emerge that is based on granting even more power to these parasites, under the guise of the need for more controls, or will states resume their own prerogative to issue their own credit on the basis of their own productivity and creativity?

So is there any hope, or is this book merely describing a predicament that is out of our control? As this is written there is a star on the horizon – in Italy. Beppe Grillo's Five Star Movement, with 8.7 million votes has become the largest single party in the Italian Chamber of Deputies. Because he is a comedian who conducted a flamboyant campaign, he has been depicted by the mass news media as a joke candidate without a policy other than upsetting the old political establishment. Yet, he does indeed have a policy, and it comprises the very ideas that are needed. He has a first-rate understanding of the financial system and what needs to be done. Dr Ellen Brown[1] who heads the Public Banking Institute in the USA, has written that Grillo's programme includes the following:

• Unilateral default on the public debt

• Nationalisation of the banks; and

• A guaranteed 'citizenship' income of 1000 Euros a month. Grillo, in a YouTube presentation cited by Dr Brown, cogently describes the debt system and the alternative:

> The Bank of Italy, a private join-stock company, ownership comprises 10 insurance companies, 10 foundations, and 10 banks, that are all joint-stock companies . . . They issue

---

1 'QE for the People: Grillo's Populist Plan for Italy', 5 February 2013, http://WebtofDebt.com/articles

the money out of thin air and lend it to us. It's the State who is supposed to issue it. We need money to work. The State should say: 'There's scarcity of money? I'll issue some and put it into circulation. Money is plentiful? I'll withdraw and burn some of it'. . . . Money is needed to keep prices stable and to let us work.

Grillo has written of the 'usurers', and 'financial powerbrokers'. His movement in Italy is the one to watch, and media/ Establishment reaction will be instructive. Grillo's 'populism' has led the media to call him the 'new Mussolini', yet there may be a deeper truth to this, if Grillo succeeds in building a movement of unstoppable momentum that will throw the money-changers out of Italy, and inspire similar movements across the world.

About the Author

Kerry Bolton holds doctorates in theology and related areas, Ph.D. h.c., and has certifications in social work studies and psychology. Fellow of the Academy of Social and Political Research (Athens) and the Institute for Higher Studies in Geopolitics and Auxiliary Sciences (Lisbon). He is a 'contributing writer' for *Foreign Policy Journal* and a regular contributor to *New Dawn* (Australia) and *The Great Indian Dream* (Indian Institute of Planning and Management).

His other books include:

Revolution from Above
(London: Arktos Media Ltd., 2011).

The Parihaka Cult
(London: Black House Publishing, 2012).

Artists of the Right
(San Francisco: Counter-Currents Publishing, 2012).

Stalin: The Enduring Legacy
(London: Black House Publishing, 2012).

The Psychotic Left
(London: Black House Publishing, 2013).